T0305911

Consumption Corridors

Consumption Corridors: Living a Good Life within Sustainable Limits explores how to enhance peoples' chances to live a good life in a world of ecological and social limits.

Rejecting familiar recitations of problems of ecological decline and planetary boundaries, this compact book instead offers a spirited explication of what everyone desires: a good life. Fundamental concepts of the good life are explained and explored, as are forces that threaten the good life for all. The remedy, says the book's seven international authors, lies with the concept of consumption corridors, enabled by mechanisms of citizen engagement and deliberative democracy.

Across five concise chapters, readers are invited into conversation about how wellbeing can be enriched by social change that joins "needs satisfaction" with consumerist restraint, social justice, and environmental sustainability. In this endeavour, lower limits of consumption that ensure minimal needs satisfaction for all are important, and enjoy ample precedent. But upper limits to consumption, argue the authors, are equally essential, and attainable, especially in those domains where limits enhance rather than undermine essential freedoms.

This book will be of great interest to students and scholars in the social sciences and humanities, and environmental and sustainability studies, as well as to community activists and the general public.

Doris Fuchs is Chair of International Relations and Sustainable Development at the University of Münster, Germany.

Marlyne Sahakian is an Assistant Professor of Sociology at the University of Geneva, Switzerland.

Tobias Gumbert is a Lecturer at the Institute of Political Science, University of Münster, Germany.

Antonietta Di Giulio is a Senior Researcher at the University of Basel, Switzerland.

Michael Maniates is Professor of Social Science (Environmental Studies) at Yale-NUS College, Singapore.

Sylvia Lorek is Chair of the Sustainable Europe Research Institute, Germany, and Adjunct Professor in Consumer Economics at the University of Helsinki, Finland.

Antonia Graf is a Junior Professor of Global Environmental Governance at the University of Münster, Germany.

Routledge Focus on Environment and Sustainability

Traditional Ecological Knowledge in Georgia
A Short History of the Caucasus
Zaal Kikvidze

Traditional Ecological Knowledge and Global Pandemics
Biodiversity and Planetary Health Beyond Covid-19
Ngozi Finette Unuigbe

Climate Diplomacy and Emerging Economies
India as a Case Study
Dhanasree Jayaram

Linking the European Union Emissions Trading System
Political Drivers and Barriers
Charlotte Unger

Post-Pandemic Sustainable Tourism Management
The New Reality of Managing Ethical and Responsible Tourism
Tony O'Rourke and Marko Koščak

Consumption Corridors
Living a Good Life within Sustainable Limits
Doris Fuchs, Marlyne Sahakian, Tobias Gumbert, Antonietta Di Giulio, Michael Maniates, Sylvia Lorek and Antonia Graf

For more information about this series, please visit: *www.routledge.com/ Routledge-Focus-on-Environment-and-Sustainability/book-series/RFES*

Consumption Corridors
Living a Good Life within
Sustainable Limits

**Doris Fuchs, Marlyne
Sahakian, Tobias Gumbert,
Antonietta Di Giulio, Michael
Maniates, Sylvia Lorek and
Antonia Graf**

Routledge
Taylor & Francis Group

LONDON AND NEW YORK

First published 2021
by Routledge
2 Park Square, Milton Park, Abingdon, Oxon OX14 4RN

and by Routledge
605 Third Avenue, New York, NY 10158

Routledge is an imprint of the Taylor & Francis Group, an informa business

British Library Cataloguing-in-Publication Data
A catalogue record for this book is available from the British Library

Library of Congress Cataloging-in-Publication Data
Names: Fuchs, Doris A., author. | Sahakian, Marlyne, author. | Gumbert, Tobias, author.
Title: Consumption corridors : living a good life within sustainable limits / Doris Fuchs, Marlyne Sahakian, Tobias Gumbert, Antonietta Di Giulio, Michael Maniates, Sylvia Lorek and Antonia Graf.
Description: 1 Edition. | New York : Routledge, 2021. | Series: Routledge focus in environment & sustainability | Includes bibliographical references and index.
Identifiers: LCCN 2020053722 (print) | LCCN 2020053723 (ebook)
Subjects: LCSH: Consumption (Economics)—Environmental aspects. | Social justice. | Social change. | Quality of life.
Classification: LCC HC79.C6 F83 2021 (print) | LCC HC79.C6 (ebook) | DDC 339.4/7—dc23
LC record available at https://lccn.loc.gov/2020053722
LC ebook record available at https://lccn.loc.gov/2020053723

ISBN: 978-0-367-74872-2 (hbk)
ISBN: 978-0-367-74873-9 (pbk)
ISBN: 978-0-367-74874-6 (ebk)

Typeset in Times New Roman
by codeMantra

Contents

Figures

Boxes

Acknowledgments

This book is the result of numerous conversations about sustainability, the good life, consumption, and justice around the March Münster Meetings. A number of sustainability scholars have participated in these annual meetings since 2012, with the authors of this book forming the core group. Given the common conviction that the idea of consumption corridors offers a necessary and intuitive means for explicitly linking questions of a good life, justice, responsibility, and ecological limits, this group composed a broadly accessible manuscript to share the corridors idea with a wider audience, including concerned citizens and practitioners around the globe. The authors are especially thankful for conversations with those who attended the March Münster Meetings, and with others along the way – too numerous to be named here. They are particularly grateful for inspiring ideas from Rico Defila, Katharina Glaab, Tom Princen, Inge Røpke, and Julia Steinberger. They would also like to thank Laura Baird Goggins for designing the figures, and the Open Access Publication Fund of the University of Münster for financial support.

1   Living well within limits

All humans want to live a *good life*. They want to live a life they value. But what does such a life look like? If you were to ask people on the street to define a good life, their answers would surely vary – by geography, age, gender, education, class, race, and access to social media, to name just a few intersecting factors. One person might respond that a good life is about having a roof over their head, running water at home, or having access to good education. Someone else might say that the good life is about enjoyment, from simple pleasures like taking regular walks in the park, to spending time with friends and family, or even traveling the world. For some, a good life might be about having a rewarding career and tallying up personal achievements. For others, commitment to community may be the defining factor.

Does that mean that differences prevail around how people achieve a good life? Actually, no. While honoring our differences as individuals, we should not lose sight of what unites us as humans. When we look beyond the surface, removing all the varied stylings and decorum, the essence of what we experience as a good life is surprisingly similar, even among individuals living seemingly different lives. At the deepest level, all human beings share certain needs that must be satisfied as a prerequisite for leading a good life. We all need access to the material necessities for life, for example, as well as a sense of belonging to some form of community and being recognized as valuable. How we satisfy these needs differs according to the places we live and the opportunities we have, but strong similarities exist when it comes to the needs themselves. And the most essential condition for living a good life, when all is said and done, is the ability to satisfy these needs.

Can you imagine a world in which all individuals living now and in the future are able to satisfy these needs and live a good life? Is such a world possible? This book invites you on a journey around a compelling vision of how a good life for all could become a reality, and how we might work together for that world.

Why do we need such a vision? If some people are able to live a life of plenty, flirting with endless possibilities of consumer goods, a vast majority barely survive, let alone live a life they value. Even people who are materially wealthy may not actually be leading a satisfying life; chasing fleeting moments of happiness may not bring about real satisfaction, and can even lead to burnout, depression, or other illnesses. A certain amount of material consumption – associated with food and water, shelter and clothes, health services, and mobility infrastructure, for example – is necessary for any human being to meet their needs. But there is also ample evidence to suggest that some consumption practices, patterns, and levels actually reduce the ability to live a good life. The lure of endless consumption opportunities, compounded by social norms and structural forces, can lead to status competition, stressful choices, time pressures, and endless debt, to name but a few ailments.

Additionally, the consumption practices and patterns of some people increasingly hamper the ability of others in this world to live a good life today, reflecting or reinforcing historical patterns of ecological and social exploitation. If certain clothing items or food products have a surprisingly low price tag, it probably means that the true costs of people's work are not being recognized. Too often, a consumer "deal" or "bargain" conceals under-paid workers and unfair work conditions. A low-cost product can also hide environmental costs, such as rainforest loss or greenhouse gas emissions. Moreover, the consumption patterns and levels of the most affluent leave a huge ecological and climate debt

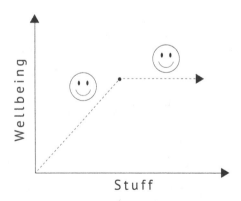

Figure 1.1 After a point, further wealth does not increase wellbeing.

to future generations. How are those who follow us supposed to be able to live good lives in this world, once we are done with it?

Thus, some kinds of consumption – too much, not enough, unequally enjoyed, environmentally or socially destructive, or divorced from wellbeing and security – are inimical to a vision of the good life for all. This is deeply ironic, since "consumption" is typically cast as essential to living well. And yet, what hinders many living in affluence from accessing a good life is the constant pursuit of a "better life." The alleged benefits of such consumerist pursuits are continuously trumpeted by advertisements in which the good life is not in the here and now, but rather achievable later, through the purchase of a new product or service. There is no question that a broad share of the global population very much needs improvements in their quality of life. For many others, however, the constant (admonition to) search for an elusive, "better" life leads to being trapped in an ever-escalating spiral of "the more, the bigger, the better," which by definition never can be good enough. Far too often, quantity takes precedence over quality.

In times of crisis, such as the pandemic that swept across the world in 2020 and 2021, we may stop and reconsider the false promises of consumerism. Such moments also show that societies can come together to determine new joint objectives, and new priorities for resource allocation and action. In this vein, it should also be conceivable for us all to agree on a vision of the good life and to work together toward the goal of enabling everybody to live it. This is the major strength of focusing on the good life, and specifically on a good life from a needs-based perspective. It allows for reflection about what we really need rather than what we wish for or desire. It also allows for a critical distinction between needs and how we go about satisfying them, and how we as a society might support the chances for needs satisfaction of others. Even more importantly, a needs-based approach to a good life illuminates the conditions that must be provided if individuals are to live a good life. And this, in turn, shines a light on needed policy and institutional reform, the (re-)organization of responsibility, and the promotion of a just society.

People have always wanted to live a good life, across the world and throughout the centuries. Societies and governments strive to support and protect the members of their populations toward that aim. Today, however, the context for these efforts has changed. We are witnessing an unprecedented global increase in urban consumers, many of whom aspire to high consumption lifestyles. At the same time, growing inequity and worrisome risks from overusing and destroying ecological resources imply that some people will never experience the lifestyles to

which they aspire. The planet simply cannot provide the ecological resources necessary for everyone to live high consumption lifestyles. Indeed, current environmental changes are already winnowing chances
for a good life. The global human society cannot endure the degree
of inequity and exploitation necessarily involved either. Not only will
this lead to much frustration and anxiety but these developments may
also erode cooperation and empathy, further worsening the situation.

*In an increasingly inequitable and ecologically full world, living well
within limits thus becomes the core challenge of our time.* Facing this
challenge means enabling every individual living now and in the future to live a life they value, while driving the institutional changes
necessary to organize ourselves with respect to these limits. All of this
is possible. Humankind, after all, has made impressive technological
advances over the decades: improved energy efficiency, the harvesting
of renewable energy resources, and the marvels of modern medicine,
to name a few. But these advances have only gotten us part way to
the good life. We need social change next to technological change. We
must nurture new institutional processes and practices for living well
within limits.

This book introduces *consumption corridors* as a means for achieving *living well within limits.* Consumption corridors describe a space
between minimum consumption standards that provide every individual with the ability to live a good life, and maximum consumption
standards that keep individuals from consuming in quantities or ways
that hurt others' chances to do the same. Such corridors combine the
pursuits of a good life and of justice within planetary boundaries. At
the same time, they offer a foundation for needed systemic change
by engaging citizens in the design and implementation of policy,
grounded in robust mechanisms of procedural justice. While a lower
limit is a starting point for discussions around justice, the need for an
upper limit is an essential next step for reasons of environmental and
social sustainability, and may make for challenging discussions. But
starting these discussions is critical.

Limits is a concept not well liked in liberal societies, where *unlimited* freedom is often extolled to be of utmost importance. And yet, we
live and thrive in a world of limits. We intuitively know that limits,
of the right type at the right time, are good for us. Individually, we
set limits on how much we eat or drink, or put on a credit card. Our
bodily and financial health would suffer if we did not. Collectively,
we embrace limits on individual freedom, via formal law or societal
norms, to protect individuals from each other or to allow the pursuit
of communal interests where they conflict with individual ones. That

is the very basis for laws, norms, and other forms of social regulation. Limits are a tool for wellbeing when they are not exploited by coercive regimes. Under the right conditions, limits are not a threat to freedom. They are its foundation.

The concept of consumption corridors thus offers a vision of how to pursue the goal of *living well within limits*. It offers a compelling vehicle to sustainability. This book is an invitation to explore the most pressing challenges facing humanity today, and to uncover how *consumption corridors* can help achieve the goal of sustainable wellbeing for all.

2 Our vision
The good life

Often, environmental and social analysts focus on threats, dangers, and damage. They highlight negatives, in terms of limited or non-renewable resources, or the impacts of excessive emissions or effluents. But what if one took the opposite approach and focused on the positives that we want to strive for? We – the authors – believe that every human being, that is you and us and everybody close and far away, wants to be able to live a good life, a life that is worth living. Given that the Earth's resources are limited and distributed highly unevenly, the core objective has to be how *everybody can live well within limits.*

Striving for this goal of living well within limits requires something different from the typical focus on threats and dangers. It requires a deep and profound orientation toward *the good life.* It requires us to ponder what the good life is, what conditions must be fulfilled for individuals to live it, and what it takes to create these conditions. Indeed, orienting our view toward *the good life* and away from threats, dangers, and damage is helpful and necessary for a number of reasons.

One is that the positivity of the vision of the good life facilitates action. Think about it. How much easier is it for us to be persistent and, if necessary, creative in pursuit of something we really want to do, compared to when we are coerced? How much more persuasive is an offer when it embraces something we care about? Motivational speakers and writers will always tell you to identify your (positive) goals first, and then go about making plans for how to achieve them. Health specialists, too, have witnessed a shift from the question "what is illness and how can it be removed?" to the question "what is health and how can it be promoted and nurtured?"

The positivity of this good-life lens relates to our search for freedom. One reason why striving for something we like or desire is powerful is that we derive additional strength from it being rooted in our freedom. We derive satisfaction from pursuing something we choose.

Indeed, the ability to design and control one's own life has been identified by many thinkers as one of the crucial needs we share as humans.

At the same time, the vision of a good life for all integrates our individual pursuit of this goal with an immediate concern for others. In other words, we can enjoy and exercise freedoms only to the extent that doing so does not impinge on others. Achieving this vision underlines both the crucial role of freedom but also the necessity of limits for this freedom to exist. Thereby, pursuing the vision of a good life for all has the potential of bridging current political divides, as it is a vision that all people can adhere to.

Beyond a concern for freedom and its limits, the pursuit of the vision of a good life for all is rooted in human inclination for empathy and desire for justice. Making the good life a goal not only individually but also at the level of societies means pursuing a vision of a world where all people, whether they are born in the Northern or the Southern hemisphere, or live on the right or the left side of the tracks, can lead a life they value. Thereby, the vision underscores the idea that the very purpose of societies is to allow its members to flourish, and it posits that all institutions of a society should serve that purpose. Making a good life a societal goal entails working at all scales, from the individual to the global, and explicitly raising these two questions: what kind of a world do people want to inhabit, and what kind of a world should be passed on to future generations? Confronting questions of what a good life consists of, how it can be achieved, and how it can be guaranteed for everybody entails exploring what really matters to humans, individually and collectively. These questions thus can launch new societal debate, helping us recognize similarities rather than differences and serve cohesion over polarization. Most fundamentally, a focus on the vision of a good life allows us, individually and collectively, to devise ways to escape the trap of "the more, the bigger, the better," and to examine how our personal understanding of the good life interacts with that of others.

Importantly, talking about a good life is not the same as talking about life being good in terms of morals, ethical rules of conduct, norms, or societal obligations. In the following pages, "the good life" refers to ideas such as quality of life, human wellbeing, and human flourishing. Nevertheless, the notions of a good life and ethical questions about rules, norms, and obligations are not completely at odds. The freedom of one individual to live a life he or she values relates to the freedom of other individuals to do the same, and brings to the fore issues of responsibility and justice. This was always the case, of course. But today, this relationship is all the more pronounced, living as we are in a world in which biophysical and social limits can no longer be denied. We can no longer ignore the fact that the pursuit of the good life can impact the chances of others to live a good life.

Pursuing the good life is about beginning with the goal of human flourishing. It does not mean that we should ignore environmental threats and dangers, or social injustice. But starting with the good life means that we set our focus straight on what is important to us, and then work our way backwards to account for limited environmental and social resources. We develop the vision of how everybody can enjoy a good life first, and then ask ourselves how that vision can become reality.

But what is a good life?

Clearly, people have different perceptions of the good life. For one person, it might be about time with the family. For another a good life could mean traveling to interesting places. And for a third it might be about a rewarding job. But what is absolutely essential for people to lead a life they value?

Scholars and thinkers across the world have pondered the good life since antiquity. They have sought to explain what the good life is and how it can be achieved. They have asked whether the focus of attention should be on individuals or the broader society. They have debated such questions in relation to virtues and morals, and rights and responsibilities. No wonder they came up with myriad answers. To some, this good life means achieving peace of mind and not being ruled by passions and desire. To others it is about living in compliance with the word of god, and observing religious duties and rules. For others it is living in harmony with nature. And for others still it is about living in accordance with human nature, focused on human capabilities and virtues.

It is impossible to present and discuss here the full range of thoughts and arguments about the characteristics of a good life. But it might be worthwhile to show the different approaches one can take and how different potential answers complement each other (for an introduction into some of these systematic differences, see Box 2.1: The good life in philosophical thought). One answer might be that a good life is the same as experiencing happiness and pleasure, and avoiding suffering and pain. In ancient Greece, *hedonism* represented such a perspective. To assess whether an individual has a good life, the good and bad feelings they have experienced would be tabulated. This calculation and the ensuing conclusion about their proximity to the good life would be entirely dependent on subjective, individual feelings.

But are feelings of happiness and pleasure, and the avoidance of suffering and pain, really sufficient or even promising for defining a good life? Interestingly, we now have evidence that people actually do not equate a good life to feelings of happiness, or to the absence of pain and suffering. Instead of weighing the balance of pleasure and pain, individuals tend to think about a good life in terms of their life being meaningful to them and therefore worth living. People distinguish, for instance, between pleasant activities and rewarding activities – the two may go together but are not always the same. Thus, someone may identify watching television as a pleasant but not rewarding activity. This distinction implies that the good life for an individual is a life that they value, independent of whether they experience feelings of happiness.

Box 2.1: The good life in philosophical thought

Several themes recur in philosophical and religious inquiries into the nature of the good life over the centuries. Reason and contemplation, moral boundaries and virtuousness, the role of body and mind, and societal participation and autonomy show up in different forms in discussions of the good life in the works of Plato, Confucius, Orunmila, Arendt, Freire, and Foucault, among others. Similarly, the question of the benefits of, if not requirement for, leading a simple or contemplative life appears in writings from Laotse, Aristotle, Augustin, and Gandhi. Beyond these common elements, there are some more or less notable differences among these thinkers. Still, one can identify certain schools of thought.

One approach takes a subjective perspective on the good life. The hedonists in ancient Greece, for instance, argued that a good life for an individual equals the experience of happiness and pleasure, and the simultaneous absence of suffering and pain. Following this definition, one could go about assessing the extent to which individuals have a good life by simply asking them about the emotions they experience. That such an assessment of a good life is entirely dependent on subjective individual feelings explains the label "subjective approaches" that today's work on wellbeing uses for such perspectives.

Subjective approaches have greatly benefitted feminist and post-colonial perspectives, as they allow for a more differentiated

(Continued)

assessment that is open to experiences from the marginalized (Spivak 1988). But they have also been criticized. Some authors argue that it is possible to be happy even in unjust or inhuman living conditions, such as a happy person living in slavery or extreme poverty, for example. Others note that happiness can be short-lived – you can be happy today but fundamentally unhappy tomorrow – making "happiness" difficult to define and support collectively (Costanza et al. 2014, Sen 2010). Brand-Correa and Steinberger (2017) also argue that in a hedonic world, achieving wellbeing relies on approaches that seek to improve people's state of mind or change their understanding of what contributes to wellbeing, with a focus on individual and subjective feelings and impressions rather than societal measures.

Unfortunately, such individualistic approaches provide little ground for capturing the relationship between the individual and society, for identifying relevant conditions for a good life, and for addressing questions of responsibility for the creation of such conditions. Accordingly, Di Giulio and Defila (2020) postulate that when it comes to societal responsibility, individual feelings of happiness cannot be the point of reference, because a community cannot assume responsibility for the happiness of its members. It can only provide the conditions for human flourishing.

In contrast to a subjective perspective on the good life, objective approaches focus on aspects beyond the individual, especially on the individual's environment. These approaches proceed from the premise that it is possible to name elements that are decisive for human wellbeing regardless of how they are experienced. This directs our focus to social and environmental contexts of individual wellbeing, thereby making it easier to posit a responsibility to ensure the opportunity to live a good life for other human beings. These approaches are also flawed, however, in that they may exclude the perspective and experience of the individual. In the worst case, they can be misused to justify coercion.

Anthropological approaches form a particular category of objective approaches to the good life. They have that name because they start from the very nature of human beings, specifically the premise that being human is inherently tied to having certain needs or needing to be able to develop certain capabilities. In this context, these approaches adopt some of the philosophical and religious notions of the good life discussed above. Aristotle's idea of *Eudemonia*, in particular, is a pivotal foundation of today's scholarly work in this area.

One influential example is Nussbaum's (1992) work on capabilities, which draws explicitly on "Aristotelian essentialism." She argues that certain capabilities, and the need to be able to develop them, are inherent characteristics of human nature irrespective of historical, geographical, and cultural contexts. Similar to other scholars applying a capabilities-based perspective, Nussbaum emphasizes that the ability of humans to develop these inherent capabilities must be the central aim of societal development, in contrast to the view of humans as productive resources that emerges in much of development policy and economics (see also Sen 1997). Politically, the capabilities perspective has served as a basis for the UN's Human Development Index (HDI) (Anand and Sen 1994). Other anthropological perspectives on the good life work with this notion of needs rather than capabilities, or combine the two (Costanza et al. 2007, Gough 2017, Max-Neef 1991).

The strength of such "eudemonic" approaches is that they consider a broad range of dimensions and determinants of individual and societal wellbeing – including social, political, economic, and cultural dimensions – and they differentiate between means and ends. With this encompassing view, these approaches offer interdisciplinary, normative frameworks that allow for a more comprehensive and differentiated assessment of individual wellbeing within society (Robeyns 2005). Rather than focusing on an individual's material resources, these approaches investigate individual capacity: the ability of individuals to meet their needs, for instance, or the capabilities that individuals command or are developing that bear on their ability to meet their needs. Resources (including social and environmental ones) in this formulation are important as a means to achieve these ends, but individual abilities to meet needs and develop capabilities determine whether people can lead a meaningful and valuable life.

Although these approaches may differ, all of them concur on three essential points: (1) A good life is not about mere survival, but rather about a life that humans value; (2) ensuring a good life is not just ensuring that people do not die, but making certain

(*Continued*)

they have the opportunity to flourish; and (3) to ensure a good life entails providing individuals with the conditions and resources needed to satisfy their needs and/or develop their capabilities.

These "objective" and, especially, "eudemonic" perspectives on the good life make it easier to identify factors influencing individual ability to live a meaningful life, while also helping us explore questions of responsibility. Most important, such approaches demonstrate that it is possible for societies to ensure that all people have an opportunity to live a good life, and to plan, organize, and adopt measures in support of this aim.

Efforts to identify decisive elements for human wellbeing must avoid paternalism, however. What people actually think must be accounted for, along with cultural and other differences in interpretations of what a good life is. In other words, it is important to avoid the danger of providing a basis for standardization and coercion toward the pursuit of improving the wellbeing of populations. While only weighing individual feelings may not be the right way to understand what a good life is, only focusing on "objective circumstances" is unlikely to be the right way either. Instead, attempts to define a good life must consider both how people actually feel about their life, and what makes life worthwhile, independent of temporary feelings. Critically, any attempt at defining a good life must acknowledge the freedom and autonomy necessary to pursue individual life plans.

Focusing on needs

Still, is it possible to identify some *needs* that all humans have and that should be fulfilled in order for individuals to be able to live a good life? Defining a good life via a focus on human needs is helpful, particularly

Figure 2.1 Some of the approaches to wellbeing.

when it comes to living well within limits. On the one hand, a needs-based approach to the good life allows us to emphasize what humans *need* to live a life they value. It thus places attention on the needs themselves as well as the conditions of their satisfaction, in a way that could be comprehensible to individuals and societal actors across nations and societal groups. On the other hand, a needs-based approach to the good life also tells us what a good life is not.

From a needs-based perspective, a good life is one where individuals have the opportunity to satisfy their human needs, and thinkers and scholars have identified certain needs as innate to human beings. While there is always some variance in how needs are identified or described, there is considerable overlap. According to most scholars and thinkers, we have, for instance, needs of subsistence, the satisfaction of which requires food and shelter, as well as needs associated with security and health, underscoring the importance of safety from violence. Other human needs suggested by thinkers and scholars are needs for affection and social relations, participation, belonging and being part of a community, reproduction, creativity, play and leisure, meaningful activities, personal development and learning, and identity.

Starting with needs, a good life is not about the satisfaction of every subjective desire individuals may have. Indeed, using a needs-based definition of the good life highlights the importance of making a crucial distinction: the distinction between "needs" and "desires." Needs are universal for humans across time and space and, more fundamentally, opportunities for satisfying these needs are a precondition of human flourishing. In this context, scholars speak of universal motivating forces, of constitutive aspects of a good life, and highlight their indispensable, irreducible, and non-substitutable nature (see Box 2.2: Needs and satisfiers).

Figure 2.2 Desires are different from needs.

Desires, in contrast, are subjective wishes. They are not crucial to an individual's ability to live a good life. That does not mean that an individual will not enjoy satisfying their desires – only that an inability to satisfy one's desires is no serious impediment to individual flourishing. Examples of such desires are the desire to drive at unlimited speed, climb Mount Everest, or live in a huge house. Desires, then, have a different standing and level of legitimacy, when societies ponder the ability of individuals to fulfill them and societal duties to ensure them. More fundamentally, it is imperative to distinguish between desires and needs in order to move beyond relativism and completely subjective estimates of wellbeing, and to identify conditions for a good life that are not solely applicable to a certain individual or group of individuals, or to any particular place and time. When using the good life as a lens for understanding better how to live well within limits, distinguishing between needs and desires is crucial.

Similarly, a focus on needs highlights the necessity to distinguish them from satisfiers. While needs are ends in and of themselves, satisfiers are what we use to satisfy our needs and desires. In other words, satisfiers are means, but not ends. When applied to consumption, this perspective clarifies that consumer goods (for example, products, services, infrastructures) are not ends in themselves, but the means for satisfying needs. Food and shelter can satisfy a need for health and subsistence, for example. Societal institutions are also satisfiers: to meet the need to participate in society, a democratic system of governance might be necessary as a means toward that end. Satisfiers tend to be culturally specific and highly contextual, in contrast to the universal nature of needs.

Therefore, when distinguishing satisfiers from needs, it becomes obvious that trying to ensure the conditions for people to live a good life means providing them with the opportunities to satisfy their needs. This is very different from saying that individuals should have

Figure 2.3 Satisfiers as distinct from needs.

opportunities to acquire and use certain satisfiers, and even more different from catering to endless desires.

Needs can be satisfied in many different ways. Traveling to interesting, far-away locations may be one way of fulfilling a need for leisure, creativity or perhaps identity or spirituality. Individuals emphasizing the importance of family for a good life may be doing so to satisfy the human need for affection or belonging. Likewise, individuals focusing on rewarding jobs may do so because the job satisfies a need for meaning, personal development, or being part of a community. Clearly differentiating between needs and satisfiers allows a distinction between the consumer goods and material as well as immaterial resources individuals may use, and the objective of a good life for which they use them – or between ends and means. Moreover, it allows an evaluation of satisfiers in terms of their contribution to needs satisfaction. Thus, a needs-based perspective on living well within limits protects us from the misstep of taking satisfiers (and potentially even the wrong satisfiers) as a point of departure; it instead directs our attention to focusing on needs and on the broader conditions for needs satisfaction.

Box 2.2: Needs and satisfiers

All need-based approaches share a main idea: human beings have a common set of needs, simply because they are human beings. The details of these needs and especially the ways in which they can be satisfied reflect cultural and historical settings, but the needs as such are universal. Needs-based approaches have been applied to a range of questions and fields, including sustainable consumption and climate change (Brand-Correa and Steinberger 2017, Gough 2017, Guillen-Royo 2010, Sahakian and Anantharaman 2020).

Needs-based approaches differ, however, around the list of needs, the number of needs identified, and considerations regarding their satisfaction (Annex 1 provides four lists of human needs employed in sustainability research). Max-Neef and colleagues (1991), for instance, identify nine needs, the satisfaction of which can be approached via a matrix. Di Giulio and Defila (2020) suggest a different list of nine needs on the basis of their potential to be "protected" in that they can be assured by collectivities. For Costanza and colleagues (2007), eleven needs are listed as contributing to quality of life.

(Continued)

Older theories about human needs also tried to distinguish different levels of needs or suggested a hierarchy of needs (Maslow 1943). The assumptions underlying such hierarchies have been disproven by empirical studies showing that this is not how people perceive quality of life, however (Banerjee and Duflo 2011). Yet, other aspects of such approaches continue to influence research. Doyal and Gough (1991), for instance, identify three needs forming a set of "basic needs," to which they add "intermediary" needs.

Needs-based approaches have the added value that they allow better insights into the qualities of satisfiers, that is, the means of achieving needs satisfaction. Max-Neef et al. (1991) distinguish among five types of satisfiers in relation to needs. First, there are violators or destroyers that impair need satisfaction. For example, the weapons industry is a destroyer of needs satisfaction for many people who are subject to the terror and violence of war. Second, there are pseudo-satisfiers, which give a false sense of satisfaction. In the United States, Juliet Schor (2000) demonstrates how the vicious cycle of work-credit-spend may make people momentarily feel exalted from a shopping experience, only to find that their needs are not truly being satisfied, as they find themselves in a spiral of debt. Third, there are such things as inhibiting satisfiers, which satisfy one need but curtail needs satisfaction with regard to other needs. Fourth, there are singular satisfiers, which satisfy just one particular need. Finally, there are synergic satisfiers, or "those that satisfy a given need, simultaneously stimulating and contributing to the fulfilment of other needs" (Max-Neef et al. 1991, 34).

More recently, in a comprehensive study on green public spaces in the cities of Asia, researchers found that these spaces satisfy multiple needs for diverse groups of people (Sahakian et al. 2020). The distinction between needs and satisfiers thus emerges as important, because it shows that sustainability is not about limiting people's needs, but rather about questioning the satisfiers that are used to satisfy human needs.

In a similar vein, a needs-based perspective on the good life reminds us to differentiate between satisfiers and resources, including biophysical and social resources. Not consuming environmental and social resources clearly is not possible. For example, people need access to drinkable water, which, in turn, requires some form of infrastructure, such as water conduits and sewage treatment plants. Even if people belong to a community of urban dumpster divers, they consume goods produced with environmental and social resources. But differentiating between resources and satisfiers allows us to evaluate satisfiers in terms of their contribution to needs fulfillment relative to the environmental and social resources they consume and affect. This is a key point for those interested in supporting a good life within limits: needs are universal, but societies can organize themselves differently to satisfy these needs with less resource throughputs and negative impacts – do better with less, in other words. The combination of the above insights on the good life derived from a needs-based perspective links consumption in terms of what resources we consume (and also waste along the production chain) to the satisfiers we choose to use to meet our needs, and to the bigger question of our needs themselves.

This perspective also reveals how consumption becomes problematic when people are no longer able to distinguish needs from satisfiers, when they consume satisfiers that are actually violators, pseudo-satisfiers or inhibiting satisfiers, or when they equate a good life with buying and possessing consumer goods. This almost inevitably leads to the trap of "the more, the better" at great environmental and social cost – and ultimately is detrimental to a good life.

The good life from a needs-based perspective, then, is a life in which individuals are able to satisfy their needs and have access to the ecological and social resources necessary for doing so. It is not a life where individuals necessarily fulfill every subjective desire, own and use any satisfier, or consume for the sake of consumption, especially when this prohibits others from living a good life. It is a life, though, that allows everybody living now and in the future to satisfy their needs within a more just world that respects planetary boundaries. It is a life that honors the vision of living well within limits.

Slipping through our fingers

This vision of a good life for all is not at all new, and it certainly is not radical. When Aristotle explored how to achieve *eudemonia* in ancient Greece, he was pondering the foundations for a good life (though, at the time, only for free Greek men). In Ecuador and Bolivia of today, *buen vivir* or living well has been inscribed in the national constitution. And in South Africa, Archbishop Desmond Tutu refers to the good life in society when writing about *ubuntu*, or the notion that "my humanity is caught up, is inexplicably bound up, in yours." Similar examples from around the world and across time abound. Truly, the good life, as an everyday aspiration by lone individuals and entire societies, is familiar terrain. It enjoys general acceptance, even if most people have not heard of terms like "wellbeing" or "satisfiers versus needs." It borders on common sense, bridging the sensibilities of conservatives and liberals.

What *is* new and radical, if we may define "radical" as a fundamental challenge to prevailing beliefs and ways of living, is how the search for the good life connects to the changing times that are upon us – and, in particular, how these changing times threaten the good life. We, the present generation of humanity, are in the midst of an urban-consumer revolution unprecedented in human history. The repercussions promise to be intense, but so are the opportunities for profound change for the better.

We inhabit an increasingly urbanized world of seven-plus billion people, heading to ten billion by 2050. The World Bank reports that the poor countries of the world, where the majority of people live, are experiencing urban population growth of more than 4%/year. Locally, such growth strains the ability of even the most efficient governments to provide basic infrastructure and services. Globally, providing basic infrastructure to the growing ranks of urban populations will, by itself, push the planet past the red-line of climate change. The capacity of critical environmental systems to support human prosperity is, as far as we know today, at its very limit, and has been passed in some areas, such as biodiversity loss and ocean acidification, with irreversible and unforeseeable consequences. The last thing humanity needs, biogeophysically speaking, is continued exponential growth in the mining, processing, and production of raw materials for new consumer products, with all the waste-production such growth entails.

Additionally, most of these new urbanites – three billion plus, by most estimates – are now scrambling aboard the bandwagon of global consumerism. Individuals across the world are easily fascinated by the "better life" as lived by the world's rich characterized by lifestyles, identities, and meaning embodied in limitless material consumption. Such "modern" or "new urban" lifestyles are usually egged on by sophisticated marketing from transnational corporations compelled to juice consumer demand and grow new markets. Spotlighted and spread through global media networks, this creation of desires and their corresponding high-consumption satisfiers are now becoming increasingly accessible to a majority of the world's population, something thought impossible just 30 years ago. And, despite the promises of a high-consumption life proffered by countless advertisements and media images, impossible it will remain, at least for many in this emerging consumer class – not everyone can live the high life of heroes and heroines in the latest Hollywood and Bollywood movies. This bait and switch of dashed expectations spawns dangerous frustrations inflamed by an economic system that has failed to deliver, given the widening gap between the haves and have nots, with a lack of real opportunities for bridging that gap.

Meanwhile, the high-end consumers of the world are not always living the idyllic life portrayed by glossy ads and chipper Instagram posts. Deepening feelings of economic anxiety are on the rise among the world's affluent (except, perhaps, for the rarified 1%) as social safety nets become frayed, a global economy creates winners and losers seemingly on whim, and an enduring sense of relative deprivation (where it seems that everyone else is doing better) becomes the norm. And yet, the global COVID-19 pandemic, the repercussions of which are still rapidly unfolding as of the time of this writing, has taught us that not all is doom and gloom. Societies have witnessed citizenly acts of kindness, solidarity, cooperation, and care. The pandemic has also exposed wide gaps in vulnerability and safety nets, however. Thus, it is an enormous challenge to keep experiences of solidarity and feelings of hope alive and to let them prime the better angels of our nature. Compassion and cooperation are so easily threatened by feelings of victimization and resentment, and fanned by opportunistic politicians, and demagogues in waiting. Accordingly, we have every reason not to let this potential interlocking explosion of consumer aspiration, dashed expectation, and deepening anxiety take hold.

Still, this risk is very real. To date, these dynamics of ecological and social destruction continue unabated. Scholars and activists point to the rapid decline of global fisheries, climate instability and flooding, droughts, growing scarcity of potable water, stalled agricultural productivity, the spread of tropical diseases, the growth of secure enclaves for the rich and insecure lives for the poor – and the list goes on. Meanwhile, current production and consumption systems are putting ever more pressure on the weaker members of societies across the globe, exploiting their every breath. But we simply cannot continue to foster the further deepening of inequalities and deprivation. *The good life is under siege!*

It does not have to be this way. The decline of the intertwined fortunes of individual and society, of person and planet is not some inevitable outcome rooted in human history or human nature. Indeed, over millennia, humanity has made impressive strides toward the good life for all. In recent decades, many people have seen real improvement in their capacity to act in the world with security, dignity, and grace.

For examples and trend lines, consider the upward global shift in life expectancy, educational levels, basic health services, literacy, and physical security documented, for instance, by the United Nations' *Human Development Reports.*

Accelerating urbanization, furthermore, may hold the key to a future firmly rooted in the good life, one where everyone participates in shaping society and gets their share, and no one shoulders the environmental or social consequences of bad behavior by others. The essential trend, here, is the depopulation of vast areas of land as humanity concentrates into cities. Relocating humanity into cities has its costs, to be sure, but one upside is the opportunity to shape patterns of production and consumption for minimal environmental impact, and maximum social harmony and justice. Imaginatively organized, city-life could provide a basis for the good life for billions of humans.

Indeed, life *can* change for the better. Humans *can* do good in the world, for themselves and each other. The good life is within our reach because of our abilities, inclinations, and achievements as creative and forward-looking bipeds, not in spite of them. To forget this truth of human potential when confronted by troubling news of social upset and environmental decline would be tragic.

But things also change for the worse, and it is the real possibility of global decline that stokes the fire behind this book. Metropolitan living that is at once socially just and environmentally sustainable remains more aspirational than inevitable. And whatever positives an urban future might offer, pronounced assaults on the natural world are unfolding now, with breathtaking immediacy. Environmental scientists calculate planetary boundaries to show, with alarm, how humanity now operates outside the "safe operating space" of the planet, how we overuse the resources provided by our planet in terms of regrowth and in terms of sinks. Threats to the good life pile upon themselves in bewildering ways as underappreciated reinforcing feedback loops kick into gear, driving a chain reaction of intensifying environmental damage. The surprising interaction of ocean waves and exposed ice-cliffs in Antarctica, for instance, promises to release staggering quantities of glacial ice into the ocean over the next several decades, inundating coastal cities at a rate previously unimaginable – and further accelerating the loss of Antarctic ice. Alas, efforts to arrest the damage, in Antarctica and elsewhere, are piecemeal at best. Even those remedies pursued with great fanfare – the Paris Agreement on climate change, to take one example – are steamrolled by a juggernaut of increased production and consumption that, by definition, defines a "healthy" global economy.

It is not just with respect to the environment, however, that things are changing for the worse. As pollution worsens in many cities around the world, the affluent shelter in their air-conditioned homes away from industrial centers with air cleaners purring and water filters on the tap. Where water service is intermittent, they purchase storage tanks for the roof; if food becomes expensive because of extremes in weather or depletion of fisheries, they import their sustenance from less affected parts of the world. And when coastal cities begin to flood, this global elite will move to equally convivial communities on higher ground. In these and so many other ways, the upper crust of humankind can insulate itself, at least for a while, from much of the environmental damage occasioned by its own consumption. The rest of humanity is left holding the bag of spotty water supplies, dirty air, expensive or unsafe food, exposure to industrial toxins, tumultuous climate, and ocean flooding.

These realities are obscured by deceptively collaborative words like "we" and "our," which are common to conversations about environmental degradation, as in "we are depleting groundwater supplies" or "our consumption of palm oil is destroying tropical forests." But the underlying realities of power and privilege are rarely so collegial or communal. A small slice of this "we" reaps the benefits of activities that devastate the environment, pushing the associated costs onto the poor, or future generations, or both. Rarely do the affluent shoulder the full costs of their consumption choices – the less powerful and un-born pay much of the bill. This fundamental unfairness means that each additional unit of growth isn't just uneconomic; it also tends to make society more unequal.

This sums to a crucial point: the unraveling of the natural world is not just an assault on future generations. It is also an inequality machine that poses grave challenges to prospects for an acceptable level of global justice. Left unchallenged, this machine will sharpen the divide between the haves and the have nots, further inflaming perceptions of injustice and marginalization by large swaths of humanity. To the dismay of many, austerity measures in Europe and continued economic dislocation in the United States after the crash of 2008/2009 created fertile ground for right-wing populism and so-called alt-right movements. But these socio-economic drivers of an often hateful politics of grievance are minor forces when compared to the power of looming environmental and social harm to erode the cooperative pillars of social life – the very pillars upon which the good life depends.

Can we be responsible for a good life for others?

A focus on the good life, we believe, offers paths of possibility to a better world. And thinking about the good life in terms of the needs individuals are able to satisfy provides a basis for identifying conditions that must be provided and resources that should be made accessible. To pursue the vision of a good life for everybody, the next logical step is to ask how meeting these conditions and ensuring the accessibility of these resources for everybody can become possible. Identifying the relevant conditions is important, as it allows actors to plan accordingly and create, support, and protect opportunities for needs satisfaction. But it is only half the game. The other important part is to discuss who the relevant actors are. Who is, can, or should be responsible for creating, supporting, and protecting these relevant conditions?

This book began with the vision of a good life for all, now and in the future. If societies wish to pursue this vision, they must accept the responsibility to provide all people with the opportunity to fulfill their needs and, on that basis, to design their lives in ways they themselves deem meaningful. Responsibility, in this sense, isn't a moral category, prescribing what is right and what is wrong, or a matter of personal choice. It's about organizing and institutionalizing global collective responsibility. It's an approach that combines the consideration of individual and collective freedom and rights with notions of individual and collective duties and obligations.

But can we really be responsible for the good life of others? Let us approach this question by exploring first what we are *not* responsible for. Despite the best intentions, no one can really be responsible for whether others experience events and moments in life as pleasurable, rewarding, or satisfying. As much as we would like to ensure that our loved ones feel happy and satisfied, and are healthy, successful, loved, and protected, we cannot – not with any certainty. We cannot control their feelings, truly shape their physical constitution, or determine how others treat them. And if we can't control these factors for our family and friends, how could we possibly assume this responsibility for individuals living far away, or in the distant future?

In truth, no one can assume the responsibility of deciding what a good life really looks like for someone else. We have neither the right to judge the paths they walk (as long as that path doesn't harm others), nor can we decide for others what a life they value should be. Each of us is responsible for designing and living our own (good) life, for figuring out what genuinely matters to us, and what that means for living a life we value.

We can and must, however, assume responsibility for insuring that individuals are able to make these assessments for themselves and act upon them. It is the very nature of societies to support their members in the pursuit of goals they cannot achieve on their own, and to allow and foster the pursuit of joint objectives. This is why we organize ourselves into communities, which balance the needs of different individuals and those of individuals and the community. As individual members of a community, we help set the stage for improving the lives of others.

This is easy to see within the family or in small communities, but it applies to a bigger community as well. Societies influence the living conditions of their members, for better or for worse, by their actions and their failure to act. Societal conditions create important contexts for individual fulfillment of needs, through the provision of healthcare, the limitation of violence, and the stewardship of environmental resources. Our grouping into societies serves physical needs around subsistence and security. It provides opportunities for participation in a community of faith to meet spiritual needs. It addresses needs related to identity, offering a sense of belonging and place as well as venues for differentiation. Other such examples abound.

Most fundamentally, a good life is unthinkable outside of a community. Humans are social animals, which is why the need for belonging and place is common to all societies. We live within social institutions – families, neighborhoods, communities, and nations – that provide psychological and material sustenance, and to which we have meaningful connections and obligations. Interacting with others allows us to develop a sense of self – this is why forced isolation is torture. And while some may tout the individualist story that we alone are responsible for our own good fortune, behind every individual action there is a collective setting within which this individual action takes place. Humans simply would not be able to survive without other humans taking care of them at some point in life; babies and children, elderly people, sick people, and all those temporarily or permanently vulnerable need others to look after them. We are always existing in and drawing on a collective.

The good life is thus more than an individual goal. It is a vision for the wellbeing of all members within a community. It says that we can and must create, support, and protect the opportunities and access to resources necessary for others to achieve a good life. This is a responsibility that expands well beyond ourselves. It is a relational form of responsibility. It links us to others.

But who are these "others" and where does our community begin and end? Traditionally, humans lived in small communities – villages or other intimate settlements – and for many this is still the case. Interestingly, this way of living still informs our thinking. When we use "community" in everyday language, we often speak of the narrow societal groupings within which we live or cognitively associate. This is the group for which we tend to accept responsibility most easily. Over time, of course, dominant forms of societal organization grew progressively larger, leading to the creation of nations, states, and the nation-states of today. But, here too, questions of responsibility and mutual obligation are frequently discussed and, in many contexts, notions of collective responsibility are accepted.

The globalized world of today complicates these familiar vessels of individual and mutual responsibility within community. Borders around communities are blurred, even in times when states go to great lengths to shelter their societies from the global flows of potentially dangerous or contagious goods and people. How countries and their citizens behave depends on what happens in other countries, and influences wellbeing in other countries. Systems of production, provisioning, and consumption are organized globally, and individuals frequently associate and interact with other individuals across borders, or literally on the other side of the globe. Individuals can also easily feel allegiance to virtual communities, without physical proximity. The idea of "community" could thus encompass an enormous group of people, especially if future generations are included, which seems mandatory to any conversation about the long-term future of humankind and associated opportunities for living a good life.

Can we be responsible for the good life of all the members of this massive community? Decades of development cooperation across the globe, often framed by the activities of the United Nations and its many programs, suggest that many would say "yes." Numerous global conferences and reports, most explicitly the 1987 Brundtland Commission's report *Our Common Future*, embody such a vision.[1] Yet, if we, as part of this community, are truthful with ourselves, we must acknowledge that notions of responsibility for the good life of individuals on the other side of the planet or years into the future are controversial, and often lack emotional or cognitive claim over our friends, family, and fellow citizens. It is thus particularly necessary to reconsider how to organize and institutionalize responsible actions toward distant others. If each and every individual living now or in the future is to have the right to satisfy human needs, then they must be provided with the necessary conditions for doing so.

Recent developments suggest that governments and the societies they represent are moving in this direction. They are beginning to accept responsibility for the wellbeing of others beyond narrow understandings of community. A familiar nation-state focus on individual wellbeing via social security, education, and health policy at the national level, for instance, is increasingly assuming an intergenerational and international focus as illustrated, to take one example, by the Sustainable Development Goals (see Box 2.3 on the good life in politics). Similarly, intergovernmental and supranational organizations – the World Bank, the European Union, civil society organizations, and even corporations – are exploring the question of the good life with renewed vigor in recent years. Reports and studies in a variety of media outlets are moving beyond expressions like "wellbeing" and "quality of life," and instead prominently featuring the less colloquial "the good life." This idea is garnering much interest among the general public, and consequently governments in different countries are working on not just understanding the nature of the good life, but also on the enabling conditions for it.

Box 2.3: The good life and related developments in present day politics

How have governments and governance systems, from local to global, envisioned and assumed responsibility for fostering opportunities for a good life for all? One answer draws on the ascendant articulation of human rights in the aftermath of the horrors of the World Wars, leading to the Universal Declaration of Human Rights in 1948. With the Declaration, nation-states through the United Nations defined certain inalienable rights, such as the right to life, equality before the law, and freedom of speech and religion, as minimum conditions for living a humane life. Second- and third-generation human rights have been agreed upon since (although their adoption and implementation at the national level is clearly lacking in certain contexts), moving the target a bit closer to conditions for not just a humane life, but for a truly good life. These second- and third-generation human rights include economic and social rights, such as the right to be employed in just and favorable conditions, or rights to food and housing.

At the national level, the welfare state created in the post-industrialization period and reinvigorated after World War II,

(Continued)

especially in parts of Europe as well as in the United States with President Roosevelt's New Deal, demonstrates efforts to create conditions for populations to meet needs and live a good life. Measures to protect individuals against threats arising from sickness or unemployment as well as to provide for education or regulate labor standards can also be viewed in this context.

In the 1960s and 1970s, a new factor relevant to living a good life moved into focus: the quality of the environment, focusing first on toxic pollutants and soon spilling over onto the preservation of natural systems. Political, scientific, and public discourse of the day increasingly linked environmental degradation to human wellbeing. Concerns about human wellbeing produced regulations focusing specifically on local air and water quality. At the same time, scientists for the first time calculated "limits to growth" (Meadows et al. 1972), which sparked debate over whether human wellbeing is truly improved by perpetual economic growth. These debates highlighted the tension between the idea, promoted in the post-war period, that mass consumption should be the final aim of any industrialized society, and the growing concern that unbridled production and consumption are fundamentally at odds with environmental limits.

In this context, it is important to recall that sentiments like Victor Lebow's famed proclamation that "our enormously productive economy demands that we make consumption our way of life, that we convert the buying and use of goods into rituals, that we seek our spiritual satisfaction, our ego satisfaction, in consumption ... we need things consumed, burned up, replaced and discarded at an ever-accelerating rate" (Lebow 1955, 8), was focused on ramping up the post-war (US) economy at a time when planetary environmental boundaries were at best a fringe concept. In other words, these ideas on wellbeing and consumption were informed by special needs and circumstances, but later came to be taken as undeniable truths valid across space and time.

The focus on human wellbeing in the context of ecological stress and the state of the planet led to the paradigm of "sustainable development," which quickly gained purchase over global political agendas in the late 1980s and 1990s, especially in the wake of the Rio "Earth Summit" of 1992. Sustainable development describes a form of development that meets human needs while sustaining natural systems so that the needs of future generations can also be met. Many environmental global summits have since been held to apply notions of sustainability to concrete political aims.

For example, the Millennium Development Goals (MDGs), a product of the United Nations Millennium Summit in 2000, promulgated eight international development goals linked to poverty eradication, environmental protection, and human rights. The UN Sustainable Development Goals (SDGs) succeeded the MDGs in 2016 and marked the shift to a broader and more transformative agenda. Its 17 goals address a broader range of ecological dimensions, while aiming to better consider the interests of marginalized groups. But more work remains. Questions persist about the operationalization and implementation of these goals, and knotty contradictions arise among some goals, especially SDG 8 ("decent work and economic *growth*," emphasis added) and SDG 12 ("sustainable production and consumption").

Increasingly, national legislative initiatives have connected to these global debates, especially emergent national proposals to combine climate change mitigation and adaptation measures with larger economic and social reforms. These plans, often referred to as a "Green Plan" or a "Green New Deal," are garnering support as of this writing, and will likely enjoy outsized attention in the post-pandemic period. Advocates argue that such initiatives will advance quality of life, resource conservation, environmental protection, and infrastructure developments by creating "green" jobs and facilitating "sustainable" investments in renewable energy and resource efficiency. But underlying visions of continual growth and an absolute decoupling of economic growth from resource use are increasingly contested. Many civil society actors and scholars alike continue to work through the possibilities for making "prosperity without growth" a reality (Jackson 2017, Victor 2008, Wiedmann et al. 2020).

Yet, despite decades of work on these themes, many people on the planet still do not have the opportunity to live a good life, and the chances of future generations to do so are plummeting. That is not to say that all efforts have failed. As noted above, policies and initiatives developed in support of social welfare and sustainable development have greatly increased the quality of life for many over the last century.

But especially in these changing times, it becomes obvious that these efforts are increasingly insufficient, for several reasons.

First, policy and governance efforts are often insufficiently aligned with the idea of a good life because they depend on poor measures of quality of life, specifically GDP (gross domestic product), which cannot accurately tally the negatives of economic growth (see Box 2.4: Quantitative indicators of quality of life). Indeed, we may have entered a phase of uneconomic growth, where the environmental and social costs of additional growth in gross domestic product exceed the benefits, a reality hidden from view by our economic scorecards. As the classic Adbusters commercial[2] reminds us, "every time a forest falls, the GDP goes up; with every oil spill, the GDP goes up; every time a cancer patient is diagnosed, the GDP goes up. Economists must learn to subtract." It is no wonder that more comprehensive assessments of economic prosperity, like the Genuine Progress Indicator (GPI), show a flattening of overall global prosperity beginning in the 1980s, even as the global GDP continues to rise.

Box 2.4: Quantitative indicators of quality of life

Scholars and practitioners have long worked with quantitative indicators of wellbeing and quality of life. Such indicators carry the promise of fruitful comparison of various strategies, both national and sub-national, to foster wellbeing, which, in turn, could offer starting points for new ideas about governance strategies and public policy. After World War II, Gross National Product (GNP) (later in the form of Gross Domestic Product or GDP per capita) became the measure most broadly used in this context.

Despite its ubiquity, the use of GDP as a measure of human wellbeing is the subject of increasing criticism (Costanza et al. 2014, Fleurbaey and Blanchet 2013, Stiglitz et al. 2010). Among the major shortcomings of GDP is its focus on market activities and added economic value, and its lack of attention to matters of income distribution. The implications of the latter are that the conditions for the wellbeing of poorer segments of societies within countries are grossly misrepresented. The consequence of the former – the focus on market activities and added economic value – means that environmental or social contributions to wellbeing outside the formal market are not counted, while activities detrimental to human wellbeing (environmental degradation, natural disasters, war, crime) may increase a country's GDP.

GDP's failings when it comes to capturing individual wellbeing are nothing new. They were pointed out early on by the index's creator, American economist Simon Kuznets, who in 1934 told the US Congress that

> the welfare of a nation can scarcely be inferred from a measure of national income. If the GDP is up, why is America down? Distinctions must be kept in mind between quantity and quality of growth, between costs and returns, and between the short and long run. Goals for more growth should specify more growth of what and for what.

While criticism of the widespread use of GDP as a measure of human wellbeing is as old as the concept itself (Abramovitz 1959), the recognition of its weaknesses has never been more significant. As a consequence, several alternative indices have emerged, the first of which was the Human Development Index in the 1990s, which combined measures of education and health with GDP to produce an overall wellbeing score for a country. Subsequent iterations included an Inequality-adjusted Human Development Index and a Gender Development Index. Annex 2 provides more information on this range of indicators.

These indexes have been faulted for an overweighting of GDP in their calculations, together with insufficient attention to the environmental dimension of human wellbeing. Other indices, many arising from governmental efforts, have sought to fill this void. Well-known examples are the Gross National Happiness Index in Bhutan, the Canadian Index of Wellbeing, and a modified Gross National Happiness scorecard in the US city of Seattle, to name just a few. At the international level, the United Nations *World Happiness Report*, first published in 2012 and covering 156 countries in 2020, might be the most prominent example.

In their attempt to infuse social, political, and/or environmental factors into conventional indicators and indexes of quality of life, scholars and practitioners have suggested several alternatives to GDP. The number and range of the measures pose

(Continued)

new problems, however, quite apart from vexing issues of data availability (Fuchs et al. 2020). Scholars and practitioners struggle with understanding what individual indicators or indexes capture, and how their respective strengths and weaknesses compare. Additionally, most alternative indicators and indexes do not offer a solution for capturing informal markets and non-market activities. Fundamental challenges also exist with integrating measures of economic wellbeing and sustainable development into one measure. As no country has yet achieved a real decoupling of resource use from economic growth, ecological and income measures tend to move in opposite directions, especially if the creation of environmental problems beyond national borders is accounted for, as it should be. The resulting inverse relationship between economic and ecological variables (see also IPCC 2018) calls into question the usefulness of a comprehensive measure covering both dimensions, since reliable interpretations of changes in the value of any such index become nearly impossible.

In sum, as economists themselves have noted for decades, we must look beyond GDP when assessing wellbeing. Indeed, any individual quantitative indicator will prove insufficient. Instead, assessments of socio-economic and political wellbeing must be employed concurrently with sustainable development indicators, but measured separately. In this vein, the Sustainable Society Index is laudable, as it distinguishes among human, economic, and environmental wellbeing (Fuchs et al. 2020). Importantly, processes of combining quantitative and qualitative assessments of wellbeing should include robust citizen involvement to foster an in-depth understanding of an individual's chances to live a good life, and to guard against the improper focus on "objective" conditions, without concern for individual experiences.

Additionally, the centrality of economic growth to national policy-making, financial markets, and corporate debt-servicing distorts our perspective of the essential goal of consumption. From the vantage point of the good life, consumption in today's world must be infused by freedom *and* constraint, and by rights *and* responsibilities. Individuals need freedom and autonomy to design meaningful lives according to their own understanding of a good life, and to choose satisfiers according to their preferences. But individuals also need to be restrained when those choices harm the opportunities of other individuals, living now and in the future, to live a good life. And this is hard to appreciate when the sole aim of consumption is framed as maintaining economic growth.

Third, more than ever, wellbeing in one country depends on what happens in other countries. With systems of production, provisioning, and consumption organized globally, individuals materially interact with other individuals across borders, and often on the other side of the globe. To gain a comprehensive picture of the factors influencing the living conditions of people, and of how individual and collective actions influence the living condition of others, we must think beyond our societal group or nation-state. And that is difficult, but necessary, since questions of a just distribution of and responsibility for opportunities to satisfy needs, and of what satisfiers and resources are made available, are global ones that extend well into the future. Responsibility, both individual and collective, to ensure that individual choices respect the opportunities of other humans to live a good life thus assumes a cross-spatial and cross-temporal dimension.

One might object that an individual human being cannot assume such massive responsibility. This is both true and false. By knowingly consuming goods produced with the help of slave labor, an individual does not cause slave labor, of course, but he or she accepts it, and thus is in some way culpable. However, a major share of the burden of organizing responsibility, especially collective responsibility, clearly rests with societies. Where one draws the line between individual and collective responsibility, and between the responsibility to foster good and avoiding the creation of harm, is unclear. But it can become clearer when we acknowledge that any answer must ensure that the individual is neither burdened with inappropriate responsibilities, nor discharged from being responsible. We also gain needed clarity when we develop and deploy conceptual frameworks to strike this balance, frameworks like consumption corridors, which will soon be discussed.

Assuming these individual and collective responsibilities might not be self-evident. In a world that was built on the abundance of cheap commodities, especially cheap energy, certain social practices and lifestyles have become normalized. To many, it is simply not clear why they should change their routines and habits, feel some responsibility for crises and suffering in far-off places, or consider new restrains on their consumption choices. Many citizens across the globe enjoy social, political, and economic freedoms and security like never before in history. Such freedom and security can easily be taken for granted, with the dynamics that produced them (oftentimes involving human and environmental exploitation) quickly falling out of sight. The altogether understandable outcome is a sense of entitlement that might lead some people to perceive attempted changes in habits, consumption choices, or domains of responsibility as an unreasoned infringement, an exercise perhaps in so-called political correctness.

Yet, in the face of complex global economic relations and power structures, it is increasingly difficult to neglect or deny our individual and collective responsibility to stop endangering others – those alive today, and those yet to be born. Credible information about our impacts on the lives of others has never been more available and plentiful. In light of this knowledge, for societies not to act responsibly is to reject the core beliefs on which most of our freedoms have been built. Freedom brings with it responsibilities, and these responsibilities include thinking about limits that help to secure established freedoms, while enabling others to realize their freedoms. For these reasons, we are obligated to parse and ponder limits to our own consumption.

Notes

1 https://sustainabledevelopment.un.org/content/documents/5987our-common-future.pdf
2 Available from online sources. See, for example, https://www.youtube.com/watch?v=0q-lEATP-9Y

3 Consumption corridors as a vehicle to pursue the good life

The idea

Consumption corridors are a powerful instrument for responsibly pursuing the good life in a world of ecological and social limits. Defined by minimum consumption standards allowing every individual to live a good life, and maximum standards guaranteeing the chance to live a good life for others, consumption corridors allow us to envision and implement the social change needed to make living well within limits a reality. Minimum consumption standards will ensure that individuals living now or in the future are able to satisfy their needs, safeguarding access to the necessary quality and quantity of ecological and social resources. Maximum consumption standards, in turn, are needed to ensure that consumption by some individuals does not threaten the opportunity for a good life for others. The space between the floor of minimum consumption standards and the ceiling of maximum consumption standards produces a sustainable consumption corridor. It is the space within which individuals may make their consumption choices freely and sustainably. It is where they have the freedom to design their lives according to their individual notions of a good life. The concept of consumption corridors combines notions of human needs, individual preferences, and freedom as the basis for a good life for all.

The very function of corridors, of minimum and maximum consumption standards, is that all individuals now and in the future can fulfill their needs. In consequence, the definition of minimum and maximum consumption standards relates directly to the question of opportunities for needs satisfaction, that is to "satisfiers." Minimum consumption standards directly follow from human needs and societal agreement on opportunities for their satisfaction. Maximum consumption standards must then be defined in ways that guarantee the ability of all individuals to meet minimum consumption standards,

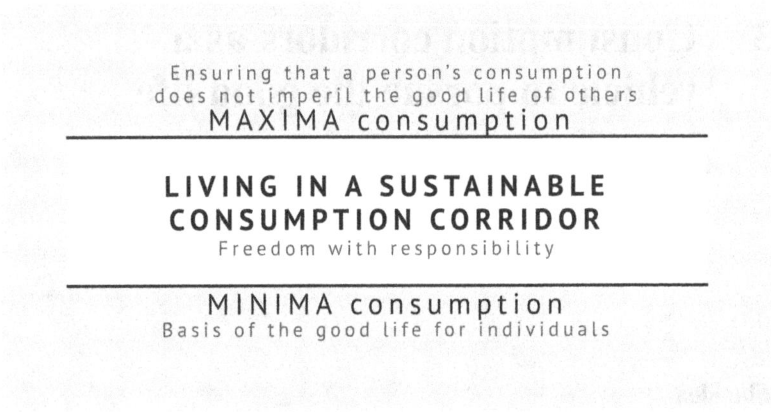

Ensuring that a person's consumption
does not imperil the good life of others
MAXIMA consumption

LIVING IN A SUSTAINABLE CONSUMPTION CORRIDOR
Freedom with responsibility

MINIMA consumption
Basis of the good life for individuals

Figure 3.1 Why consumption minima and maxima are necessary.

depending on the definition of needs and agreement about opportunities as well. How to satisfy these needs can be a question of personal choice, as long as maximum consumption standards are not violated. In other words, "satisfiers" do not receive the same kind of protection via consumption corridors that "needs" receive (as discussed in Box 2.2: Needs and satisfiers).

Box 3.1: The origins and further evolution of consumption corridors as an idea

The concept of consumption corridors emerged from a large, transdisciplinary research program funded by the German Ministry for Education and Research, entitled "From Knowledge to Action – New Paths towards Sustainable Consumption." More than a hundred researchers and eighty collaborating partners participated in this primary program, and their work was complemented by a parallel research project in Switzerland tasked with coordinating and promoting exchanges and synthesis among the research teams, and transferring key findings to the public. These efforts produced eight recommendations, or "consumption messages," for the implementation of sustainable consumption across society (Blättel-Mink et al. 2013). The corridors message, which sketches the conceptual foundations and reasoning behind consumption corridors, was among these eight.

Since then, corridors have been the focus of a number of research efforts and working groups. In 2018, a series of scholarly panels on consumption corridors convened at the international conference of the Sustainable Consumption Research and Action Initiative in Copenhagen. In April 2019, an international workshop at the University of Geneva further developed the concept, leading to a special issue devoted to consumption corridors in the journal of *Sustainability: Science, Practice, and Policy.*

Additional scholarly inquiries into consumption corridors have pushed the concept further. Some publications have elaborated on the norms and ideas underlying the concept and their fit with the normative paradigms and perspectives prevailing in today's Western democratic societies (Defila and Di Giulio 2020, Di Giulio and Fuchs 2014, Gough 2020). Others have explored the meaning of corridors in specific empirical contexts (Godin et al. 2020, Jäger-Erben et al. forthcoming, Sahakian and Anantharaman 2020). A third group of studies has asked questions about the design and implementation of corridors, and accompanying structural changes in society (Fuchs 2020, Fuchs et al. 2019).

Both minimum and maximum consumption standards are central to the vision of enabling every individual living now or in the future to pursue a good life. Again, minimum consumption standards are necessary to ensure that every individual can access the social and ecological resources necessary to satisfy their needs. Importantly, this access is not just a question of quantity but also of the quality of resources. Maximum consumption standards are crucial for ensuring that we do not destroy the ability of others to achieve minimum consumption standards. Integrating a focus on minima and maxima is the basis for addressing questions of justice in a more profound and comprehensive way than a sole focus on the necessity of minima. Indeed, maximum consumption standards enforce a powerful message about justice, which is a central goal of consumption corridors.

Minimum and especially maximum consumption standards cannot be defined once and for all. They must instead be periodically readjusted according to social and ecological developments, new insights, and changing value systems. Human-nature interaction is constantly evolving, as is our understanding and valuation of relevant ecological and social limits. Moreover, the translation of needs into satisfiers must be culturally and historically specific. Similarly, the specific level of resource consumption via a given satisfier will change with techno-logical and societal innovations.

Note that the concept of consumption corridors does not imply that everybody will or should consume exactly the same quantity and quality of resources. Justice in the context of consumption corridors means that every person deserves access to a defined minimum level of ecological and social resources necessary to be able to live a good life, solely because they are a human being (what scholars call a natural-law-based perspective on justice). In this way, consumption corridors promote justice as a fundamental condition and basic norm for struc-turing how humans live together. The concept understands humans to be social beings and assumes that living within societies is associated with collective responsibilities, which includes the acceptance of cer-tain limits on individual freedoms.

The idea of consumption corridors is not alone in its attempt to pro-vide a strategy for a joint pursuit of wellbeing, justice, and responsibil-ity in a world of limits (see Box 3.2: Related concepts in science). The idea of consumption corridors is unique, however, for placing the link between the good life and consumption at the center of such a strategy, and in making that link via a needs-based perspective on the good life against the backdrop of limits. Both lower and upper consumption limits are justified by the good life, thereby refocusing our attention on the essence of human aims and ambitions. Because of this focus, the concept of consumption corridors naturally emphasizes the ecological and societal conditions for wellbeing in the context of consumption, thus forcing us to take a more comprehensive look at demands for dif-ferent resources and the implications thereof.

The concept of consumption corridors thereby allows for a deeper appreciation of the idea of sufficiency, which increasingly arises in today's scientific and political debates about sustainability. In the context of corridors, sufficiency is understood as "enoughness" in the sense of enough for each individual, and enough for everybody. Suffi-ciency is about life between minimum and maximum standards; it is not about unguided renunciation or promoting asceticism.

The idea of consumption corridors is also operationally advanta-geous, in that it allows us to envision the existence of several corridors defined by different resources, consumption domains, or satisfiers, and potential transits among them. Finally, the concept makes the need for a dynamic nature of such corridors clear from the outset, meaning that a corridor will likely expand or contract over time. This highlights the importance of a reflexive, deliberative process that periodically evaluates and redefines the upper and lower limits of the

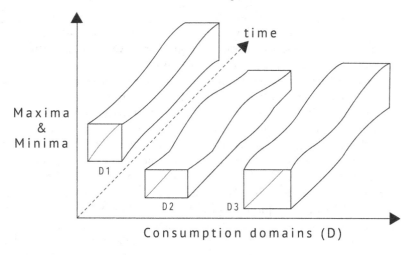

Figure 3.2 Consumption corridors changing over time.

corridors, whenever conditions or knowledge regarding resource demand or availability change. This capacity for frequent recalibration can reinforce the fundamental commitment of consumption corridors to a vision of a good life for all living now, and in the future.

Box 3.2: Related concepts in science

In addition to consumption corridors, other concepts exist that integrate ideas of wellbeing, justice, and limits. Just like the corridors concept, they build on a range of notable publications (Jackson 2005, Schor 1998) that bring questions about consumption and wellbeing to the forefront of sustainability research and debate. These include the widely acknowledged notion of a "safe and just operating space" (Dearing et al. 2014, Rockström et al. 2009). Raworth (2017) has also gained prominence with the illustrative notion of "doughnut economics," which relates planetary boundaries to social foundations, and highlights the urgent need to develop an environmentally safe and socially just space for humanity. Likewise, Opschoor's (1987) concept of "environmental space," which was taken up by Friends of the Earth Europe (Spangenberg 2002), links the existence of limited natural resources to ideas of justice and the good life.

(Continued)

Other science-driven developments that connect to consumption corridors include work on upper or lower limits. With respect to upper limits, research focuses on the dimensions, political feasibility, and implications of maximum incomes (Gough 2017, Neuhäuser 2018). With respect to lower limits, a body of provocative inquiry explores socio-technical systems of provisioning, linking energy services to basic needs (Brand-Correa et al. 2018) or universal basic services (Coote and Percy 2020). This literature also studies the material necessities for a good life, reinforcing the idea of minimum levels of socially acceptable consumption while also implying the need for maximum limits (Millward-Hopkins et al. 2020, Rao and Min 2018).

Not unlike the concept of sustainable consumption corridors, these investigations accept the urgent need to integrate the pursuit of sustainability with social justice. Many if not most, moreover, draw on spatial metaphors to frame arguments and illustrate strategies for change. As noted above, however, the concept of consumption corridors stands apart by placing the link between the good life and consumption, and specifically the good life and upper and lower limits for consumption, at the center of its strategy for change.

Limits are already out there

Can you imagine a world without limits? Having to navigate a city without any limits on how people drive, for example? Or no limits on what harm we may do to others? Societies need limits to allow the common pursuit of individual and societal wellbeing. The limits set by states during the COVID-19 pandemic to protect public health, and especially the health of the most vulnerable segments of societies, are a case in point. There is, in fact, something comforting about limits, especially if citizens come together to develop and implement them.

In like fashion, limits to consumption are not fanciful ideas in service of the good life. They exist in the here and now, the product of common sense and compassion, in part because consumption limits arrived at collectively are more often freeing than coercive. In our societies, we have agreed – sometimes implicitly, but oftentimes explicitly – on a plethora of upper and lower limits to consumption.

Let us start with examples of lower limits, which are probably better known. One is the Social Protection Floor developed internationally by the International Labour Organisation (ILO) and UNESCO. This floor is intended as a lower limit for guaranteeing access to basic social security services. Internationally and nationally, such guarantees are often expressed in terms of minima, such as access to basic health care, including maternity care, or basic income security, including revenue for the elderly or disabled. An operationalization of minimum consumption levels considered necessary are "consumption baskets" used to calculate the level of social security payments at the national level, or more recently the concepts of "basic income" or "universal basic services." Societies also agree on minimum levels for education provided by public resources (to the extent that education systems are publicly funded). Such agreements typically entail specifics on the minimum amount of school years that should be required for children and publicly funded, as well as on acceptable student-to-teacher ratios.

Societies also embrace consumption *maxima*. Consuming alcohol beyond a certain level when driving is punished in many societies. Such rules exist for safety reasons, of course, to protect not just the driver but also the lives of others. They thus function in a manner similar to the maxima of consumption corridors: their intent is to ensure the ability of others to live a good life. Likewise, limits are set on what property owners may do with their property – for example, limits on size, location, and use of a building that one constructs and, in many countries, the maximum amount of energy that can be consumed (via energy efficiency standards). Restrictions may also apply to how many wells you may dig or how much water you are allowed to use per day, how many trees you may harvest, or how much or what kind of trash you may burn on your property (if at all), given water, biodiversity, or air quality concerns. These restrictions highlight examples of consumption maxima defined in relation to scarcity of resources, in terms of quantity or quality. In this vein, the use of private cars was restricted during the oil crises of the 1970s, and the speed limit has been reduced in some countries temporarily or permanently due to ecological concerns.

Some limits exist for the individual, others for the collective. Singapore sets a maximum limit on the number of motorized vehicle licenses available, which grows stricter over time. Major cities such as Amsterdam, Barcelona, and Venice are beginning to impose limits on tourism, with restrictions ranging from the number of individuals to the number of cruise ships allowed per day. And in Switzerland, a law passed in 2015 in response to speculative housing development in the picturesque Swiss Valais region sets a limit on the proportion of residences in secondary housing – 20% is the maximal limit – to protect the communities in the villages and towns. The law is currently contested, as some feel it advantages those who have already invested in secondary homes; it also does not lead to a more equal distribution of secondary homes. But as a direct result of this law, rapid and speculative housing development in some Swiss regions has been blunted, and halted altogether in areas like the Valais.

While maximum and minimum consumption limits are common, combining the two is decidedly less so. There nevertheless are examples where consumption minima and maxima have been defined in the same area even if not necessarily in combination. Box 3.3 describes relevant governmental measures as well as interesting research into housing size. Even though there is a noteworthy lack of policies and regulations addressing upper limits in this area – in contrast to the quantity and breadth of measures focusing on energy efficiency aspects – ideas about appropriate limits show up in one way or another in the context of welfare payments, for instance.

Box 3.3: Housing size and limits

In many countries, household energy use is among the core drivers of consumer environmental impact, next to mobility and food (IGES 2019, Lorek and Spangenberg 2001). Policies and NGO campaigns have tried to address this impact in a variety of ways: prescribing, for instance, standards for the energy efficiency of buildings, fostering the energy efficiency of heating systems, or – less commonly – appealing to households to lower average room temperatures. The growth in living area per person has rarely been addressed (Wilhite 2016), however, despite increases over the last decade. Per capita living space in new single-family homes in the United States, for instance, almost doubled between 1973 and 2015 (Perry 2016). Indeed, next to the increasing number of single households, the desire for larger homes and more, bigger, and better appliances is a key driver behind increasing household energy consumption (Cohen 2020, Sahakian 2019). Here, the impact of rebound effects becomes visible (see Box 4.1: Why easy wins for more sustainable consumption won't be enough).

What lies behind this trend of increased living space per person? One driver is the proliferation of possessions across the middle- and upper-classes. Sahakian (2019), among others, documents the explosion of household goods and appliances, linked in part to shifting perceptions of "high status" interior design. Additionally, individual living space tends to increase along with age and career stage, irrespective of family size. The trend of increasing home sizes may also be a function of the often overlooked negative impacts of larger domiciles, such as the energy needed to heat or cool additional space, or the additional time (or money) needed to clean the home (Shove and Warde 2002). In many instances, moreover, larger homes are a consequence of status-driven consumption, where so-called McMansions confer additional status to their owners – until, that is, McMansions in one's social group become the norm, producing the social need for even larger, more elaborate homes (Frank 2000, Pinsker 2019). Against this background, enforcing upper limits on living size per person would appear to be both wise and necessary. At the same time, such a step makes visible the fundamental social change implied by challenging "bigger is better" as a normative aim.

So, what would a perspective of consumption corridors for the good life tell us about the size of our homes? Most fundamentally, it would have us ask how large a home is sufficient to meet our needs. It could also help us see and challenge the practices and norms driving us to larger homes, while highlighting the negative impacts of ever-expanding domiciles on the chances to live a good life.

Minimum housing consumption standards are familiar and accepted – there is nothing earth-shaking here. For instance, welfare systems in many countries operate with a standard in terms of square meters per person as a basis for rent support. An international standard developed by the International Code Council (ICC) sets a minimum requirement for residential space of 13.9 m² for the first occupant and 9.3 m² for each additional resident. On the scholarly side, Rao and Min (2018) apply a needs-based approach and identify minimum floor space as a universal satisfier in the context of living – next to adequate lighting, basic comfort in terms of temperature and humidity, adequate and accessible water supply, and safe waste disposal – and calculate it to be a minimum of 30 m² for up to three persons plus 10 m² per additional person. The Swiss decree on minimum

(Continued)

flat size requires 40 m² for a single-person household and 10 m² more for each additional household member.

When it comes to upper limits, however, examples are more scarce. Yet notions of appropriate upper limits exist with respect to rental benchmarks (*Mietrichtwerte*) in welfare states, such as Germany, for instance. Here, rental support to welfare recipients is based on a combination of square meters per person (50 m² for a single person and 15 m² for every additional one) and local market rates for rents/m². Additionally, a growing number of research projects around planetary limits have experimented with upper limits on per capita floor space, suggesting 20 m² for a "one planet lifestyle" based on resource availability (Lettenmeier 2018), 30 m² per capita as part of a scenario limiting global warming to 1.5°C (Grubler et al. 2018), and 35 m² per capita for Germany in discussions about equity, justice, and social capital (Bierwirth and Thomas 2019).

Most of these analyses do not adopt a needs-based perspective on the good life. Instead, they usefully turn our attention to the energy needs of people and the ecological benefits of trimming residential floor space per capita. In doing so, they reflect a growing social acceptance of the virtues of smaller living areas, and reinforce a number of fascinating trends toward downsizing of living areas. For instance, an increasing interest in urban living among younger generations is normalizing smaller domiciles. But there is also the tiny house movement in the United States, which dates back to the 1970s. It has been enjoying a renaissance since the financial crisis of 2007/2008, and will likely see even more attention in the post-pandemic period. This push toward smaller homes is emerging in many cities and countries around the world as planners, architects, and citizens experiment with micro apartments, co-living spaces, vertical villages, communal or multi-generational housing projects, and projects combining small flats with generous common-use spaces like cafés, gyms, and recreation areas (Lorek and Fuchs 2018).

The specification of upper consumption limits for per capita floor space is not the only possible strategy for arresting the growing per capita housing footprint. Just as important would be the reversal of practices, policies, and laws that promote larger homes. Public loans for energy efficient buildings could be based on energy per capita consumption rather than square meters, for instance, and public support for new residential buildings could be restricted to a maximum size per person. Likewise, a range of associated regulations and practices could be reconsidered, such as how architects' fees are calculated – often based on the total budget, so the bigger the better in terms of service fees. These examples show that regulations that foster smaller per capita floor sizes would not present an unprecedented intervention into the "freedom" of homeowners, but instead a redirection of priorities toward collective and societal goals – for the good life for all.

Upper and lower limits are also sometimes defined by individuals organized in initiatives or associations, including but not limited to ecovillages and transition towns. The 2000-watt society is one example. Emerging in Switzerland in the 1990s, the idea is that energy consumption per person must be limited to two kilowatts (or 2kWh per hour, equal to 48 kWh per day) to guarantee everyone on the planet access to an acceptable level of energy consumption. The Swiss federal government has included the target of 2000 watts per person in its Sustainable Development Strategy, and the citizens of Zurich City voted in 2008 to include the objectives of the 2000-watt society in their municipal regulatory system, providing direction to the city's energy strategy.

The possibility and prevalence of upper and/or lower consumption limits differ across policy fields. In the area of energy consumption, this acceptance is perhaps the broadest. There is clear consensus that a minimum amount of energy consumption is necessary to meet basic human needs, such as energy for cooking, lighting, and indoor heating in cold climates or cooling in hot ones. When these minima are not met with reliable and affordable energy, as is the case for billions of people, energy poverty arises. Energy poverty is especially apparent in parts of India and other spaces in the Global South, where rural electrification remains limited, but it also exists in many regions of so-called industrialized countries. The dumping of shoddy, energy inefficient appliances from wealthier countries into poorer ones complicates matters, as do political dynamics within many countries that steer energy-infrastructure investments toward the needs of the affluent, leaving the poor high and dry.

The appropriateness of limits arises in other domains of consumption as well. One notable trend is the emergence of "no flying" and "flying less" initiatives that respond to the ecological impact and social inequality of flying: wealthier people fly more that others, but the resulting carbon emissions affect everyone, especially those with limited resources who are typically more vulnerable to climate disruption. A variety of initiatives, citizen groups, universities, and environmental organizations are fostering individual commitmentsto avoiding short flights or giving up flying for a year or more. One relevant effort[1] organized by academics brings together individuals and organizations from Germany, Switzerland, and Austria who vow to avoid flights for distances under 1,000 km, for instance.

Extending the view to the mobility sector more broadly, resource savings from limits to flying could be distributed to other transport systems to promote a range of alternatives, especially train travel. Limits could also be considered at the local level around other forms of mobility. Municipalities, for instance, could provide shared car fleets, with a kilometer per person limit, rather than allow access to private cars. Once collectively negotiated with reference to human needs, such mobility limits could be easily governed and sanctioned, though they would need supporting infrastructure investments and attention to social-justice issues to ensure that diverse mobility needs – both in the urban centers and in peri-urban or rural communities – are met.

Similar debates arise around food, especially meat and (to a lesser extent) dairy products. The idea of "meat-free days" has been embraced around the globe. Started in memory of the Indian educator Sadhu Vaswani in the 1980s with the campaign for International Meatless Day, "Meatless Mondays" or "Veggie Thursdays" have been introduced in cities in Belgium, Finland, and Brazil, and in schools and universities across the United States and Canada. Although far from overall consumption limits, these efforts show that relevant ideas about upper and lower limits already exist in everyday life.

In a world of growing social inequity and increasing ecological fragility, limits to consumption that translate into greater wellbeing for more people are necessary. Everybody needs to have access to what they require to be able to live a good life. At the same time, nobody should consume so many resources that they hurt other individuals' chances to live a good life. Fortunately, societies already know how to construct limits for the benefit of all.

The limits discussed here, and others like them, are not, however, consumption corridors. They have arisen from a confluence of what are perceived to be individual, societal, or ecological necessities, by communities and governments that have some idea about "quality of life" and social equity. But these considerations usually focus more on satisfiers than on needs, and almost always ignore the needs of others around the globe, and of future generations.

Building certification schemes illustrate the problems that arise when needs are not sufficiently accounted for, and when more attention is given to satisfiers than needs. For example, the shelter of a home is one way of feeling safe and protected, and an "efficient" building suggests that these needs can be satisfied with less energy. But oftentimes, such buildings are designed without accounting for the diverse ways in which people satisfy their needs and perform everyday life activities. The result is what is known as the "performance gap," whereby the actual energy savings are much lower than planned for in the design phase.

Thus, while the concept of consumption corridors is new, lower and upper limits to consumption are not. The idea of corridors brings a new dimension and value to such limits that societies may ponder, debate, and decide. It draws our attention to human needs as a starting point for this process, asking us to distinguish needs from satisfiers and unlimited desires, and to consider the needs of all people now and into the future. Rather than constraining us, such limits offer the freedom to live a good life while preserving the chances of others to do the same.

What kind of processes are needed?

Examples abound of societal limits on consumption that support human-needs satisfaction, social justice, and environmental sustainability. How, though, do we move beyond these inspiring examples? How do we begin the project of designing and implementing consumption corridors that will make societal limits on consumption more the norm than the exception? The answer is that consumption corridors must be envisioned and developed via lively democratic debate within robust forms of civic participation. Participating citizens must be diverse in terms of gender, education, income, age, and family status, and they must experience the deliberative process as fair and transparent. Varied groups must be involved, representing diverse fields of interest and action, from environmental and consumer-rights organizations, to regional development planners and municipal actors, to solidarity- and circular-economy promoters, to groups engaged in human rights activism. The legitimacy and effectiveness of the upper and lower bounds of consumption corridors demands nothing less.

A focus on the participatory requirements of consumption corridors is a useful reminder of the democratic necessity of promoting citizen competence through accessible and inclusive public debate about the kind of society we want and the goals we strive to achieve. In this way, the development of consumption corridors differs markedly from elite-driven attempts to reframe consumer choices or introduce "nudging" incentives to shift buying patterns. Both are strategies-of-choice among many public officials involved in national sustainable consumption programs, especially programs that engage people in their role as consumers, and push consumers to be marginally more sustainable with little transparency. The participatory processes essential to corridor development and articulations of the good life run in the opposite direction. They view people primarily as citizens, focus on helping individuals flex their citizen muscle, guide people in negotiating their ideas of a good life with others, and allow citizens to jointly recognize and decide upon necessary pathways for change.

To this end, negotiations at the societal level around consumption corridors must engage individuals in civil conversation about what they cherish, and what opportunities they envision for humans living today and in the future. These conversations will be most effective when they occur across different contexts and cultures, spanning all societal sectors, regions, ideological characteristics, and environmental conditions. Both theory and practice around such deliberations assure us that they are capable of producing a workable consensus on questions of consumption, limits, and the good life that would be impossible under more elite-driven, top-down approaches. People, after all, are more accepting of decisions and rules that their peers or they themselves have designed or vetted. But it is much more than a question of acceptance. It is a question of how corridors fit with the opportunity for everybody, living now and in the future, to live a good life, and the essential role that everyday people must play in developing and envisioning solutions to complex problems.

We do not claim that deliberative community conversations for justice or sustainability have been perfect in recent practice. They often lack representativeness, and thus can exacerbate existing power asymmetries. This is likely why, around the world, scholars, practitioners, and activists are fervently working to improve the democratic quality of deliberative processes, focusing especially on what is called transdisciplinary research – forms of research that integrate science and practice, and that bring scholars and citizens together in the design and implementation of effective responses to social problems. These are exactly the sort of processes required by consumption corridors.

The encouraging news is that scholars and practitioners have interrogated these issues for decades, from Granada to Medellín (see Box 3.4: Citizen engagement in relation to limits, needs, and wellbeing). Their insights suggest a three-stage process for the design and implementation of consumption corridors.

The first stage centers on deliberations about problem perception and visions for the future, especially as both relate to ideas about the good life. It is hard to deny that certain visions of the future enjoy the backing of powerful actors – those that offer economic growth as the sole response to all social and environmental ills, or avidly promote consumer lifestyles as an ultimate goal. It is important to cut through this clutter to agree on what we mean by the good life, and thus to agree on a shared vision moving forward.

To further the pursuit of a good life for all, and to lay the foundation for designing consumption corridors, individuals working within community could explore the following questions:

- What is the problem? What opportunities and challenges characterize your life? Where do they come from? What do you wish would change for you and what would you keep the same? Who, in the world that you inhabit, has the most power to keep things the same, and who has the most power to change things?
- What are needs? How does this differ from desires and the means of satisfying needs? How do these needs differ from what we hear in the media or what we might have been brought up with or taught to believe?
- How do we feel about limits? What are existing examples of upper and lower limits to consumption (for example, health, safety, education)? How did they come to pass, by whom, and through what process? What are the strengths and weaknesses of these approaches? Who gained and who lost from these processes?

These will not be easy discussions. People come with their own baggage, experiences, and histories, and it is often difficult to untangle how and why people identify problems and envision solutions. In this effort, we need scholarly and scientific expertise *and* insights from the lived experience of citizens and non-governmental organizations – the joining of what can be called certified and non-certified knowledge within interdisciplinary collaborative processes. After all, many of the critical issues facing humankind today cannot be understood from a single perspective. Tapping multiple views for the design of consumption corridors means striking a balance between getting the best available scientific and technical knowledge on board, while also recognizing the limits of science by honoring practical knowledge about everyday life, routines and practices, and competing societal and cultural contexts.

These varied forms of knowledge and expertise are all the more necessary in the second stage of conversation, which focuses on linking human needs to available resources, both biophysical and social. A major question to be resolved is how satisfiers, which depend on societal and ecological resources, fulfill needs. Although deliberations on these questions can be inspired by certified or non-certified expert knowledge about needs and satisfiers, resource consumption, and ecological and social dynamics, none of this works without robust conversation among citizens. As described in a prior chapter, scholars and thinkers have suggested sets of needs as inherently human, but they have not provided a single, definitive list of needs. Additionally, needs can be met with different satisfiers and these differ across cultures, time, and space, as well as in terms of their potential to contribute to the satisfaction of needs (see Box 2.2: Needs and satisfiers).

Devising a societal goal of "living well within limits" therefore depends on broad, integrated, and structured debates about needs and appropriate satisfiers. Tying limits to needs and deliberating and deciding these limits in society are crucial for three reasons: (a) to ensure that upper and lower limits contribute to the good life for all, (b) to allow for the meaningful integration of limits into the everyday practices of collectives and individuals, and (c) to provide the foundation for the societal acceptance and democratic legitimacy of these limits. Because who can argue with a policy or process that is aiming for need satisfaction for all?

At this second stage, the following questions could be discussed to advance debate and implementation:

- What is an appropriate list of needs? What lists of needs are relatable and workable, and help uncover individual needs, while allowing for societal planning for provisioning opportunities for needs satisfaction (see Annex 1 for examples of different lists).
- What are the relevant "satisfiers" for meeting needs? What socio-technical systems, products and services, infrastructures, institutions, and policies are necessary for satisfying these needs? One approach would be to map the socio-material system of a consumption domain, such as mobility, food, or household energy use to gain a clearer understanding of that system. What actors are involved, who is included or excluded, and what social and political power dynamics are most apparent? What social norms, rules, regulations, or other controlling mechanisms exist? What does the materiality of that consumption domain look like, in terms of infrastructures and products? What skills and competencies are needed?

• What are the important social and environmental impacts and considerations? If needs are universal, the means of satisfying them are anything but. A car or a bike might satisfy the same needs, but a bike, in its usage phase, consumes no fossil fuels and releases no carbon emissions. Decisions can be made on which "satisfiers" have fewer negative social and environmental impacts over others.

The range of all possible options for satisfying needs for all people is a consumption corridor. It is defined by setting a minimum level of consumption allowing individuals to satisfy their needs, and a maximum consumption level that avoids negative social and environmental impacts that would threaten the chances of other individuals to meet their minimum consumption levels. The essential task is to determine how much of a good or service is enough to address "need satisfaction." Setting lower and upper limits to consumption, or creating a sustainable consumption corridor, is ultimately about sufficiency, about deciding how much and what kind of access to societal and ecological resources must be ensured to meet needs for all. Deliberations between certified and non-certified experts are necessary to answer these questions, by translating these minima into resource consumption indicators and calculating relevant maxima on that basis, drawing on existing knowledge of ecological and societal limits. As discussed above, first estimates for consumption corridors in specific areas have been developed and could provide a starting point for lively, interactive, and inspiring conversation.

Discerning how best to implement, evaluate, and periodically readjust corridors is the goal of the third and final stage of debate. Designing and implementing corridors will not be easy or straightforward. It entails accounting for different scales of action, varying focus areas for that action, and interdependencies among sectors and geographic areas in an increasingly interconnected world with a diversity of people and contexts. A balance must be achieved between defining consumption corridors in too much detail or too little, knowing that corridors for the same set of needs and satisfiers may vary substantially within and among different contexts and cultures. Consequently, an on-the-ground transition to corridors might best be thought of in smaller units or building blocks, rather than immediate, all-encompassing change. One benefit of this incremental approach is greater sensitivity to the perspectives, historical trajectories, and socio-cultural distinctions of specific regions and communities.

At this third stage, the following questions could usefully support the definition and implementation of consumption corridors:

- What specific upper and lower limits to consumption are necessary? The results that come about from setting consumption corridors must lead to limits that can be agreed upon.
- How can consumption corridors be implemented? At what scale and with what resources? Who are we with? Who are we against, in terms of shared and competing interests?
- What must change? What is preventing or hindering the possibility for change? How can change be further supported?
- How can implementation be assessed and evaluated? How and when will the corridors be reassessed and, if necessary, adjusted?

The questions running through these three stages of conversation and debate are large and complex. Some may call them utopian, and too demanding of "ordinary" citizens. We the authors disagree. There are many examples of successful efforts to engage citizens in such deliberations, including governance initiatives in which people collaboratively agree on wellbeing indicators, and citizen-led initiatives to discuss limits in relation to carbon emissions, to name a few (see Box 3.4: Citizen engagement in relation to limits, needs, and wellbeing). These efforts occur at the local level (for example, participatory budgeting within many cities around the world), and the national (around, for instance, the United Nations Sustainable Development Goals). Real-world experience, full of promise, exists.

The overall process of designing corridors is likely to hold fascinating but also challenging insights. What happens when people start asking themselves what they truly need to live a good life? Or how one best links "needs" to "satisfiers" to allow others to live a good life, now and in the future? And what do we realize when we ask ourselves what or whom is hindering need satisfaction, and who or what is supporting it?

It is likely that these queries will underscore the importance of changing habitual ways of being and doing, both individually and collectively. They will also highlight the importance of redesigning institutions, processes, and infrastructures – which will lead to more questions about policies, regulations, infrastructures, and social institutions for transitioning to new ways of doing. The cascade of insights, conversations, and questions that will surely follow will be challenging. None of it will be easy. And yet this is exactly the kind of productive turmoil that will lead to the fundamental social shift that is needed in pursuit of a good life for all.

Let us work to find a starting point for discussions and processes toward consumption corridors at the local, regional and, perhaps, national levels. While none of us can design and implement consumption corridors individually, we can become involved in societal debates that jump-start conversations about upper and lower limits to consumption. If we wish to create a world in which everybody can live a good life, let us act bravely and dare to ask what is needed and how much is enough – for today and into the future.

Box 3.4: Citizen engagement in relation to limits, needs, and wellbeing

Societal actors are pursuing multiple avenues to identify human needs in relation to wellbeing (as discussed in Box 2.2: Needs and satisfiers, and with select lists provided in Annex 1). In the academic arena, transdisciplinary approaches are increasingly prevalent, in which diverse populations participate in the analysis and framing of relevant problems, and in the creation of new knowledge.

One recent example is research that drew on precariously employed or unemployed young people in Granada (Spain) to understand how "needs fulfillment" is a more useful approach to social-welfare policies than simply prioritizing economic growth (Guillen-Royo et al. 2017). Another example comes from Sahakian et al. (2020), in which citizens in four cities (Chennai, Metro Manila, Shanghai, and Singapore) were asked to relate "going to the park" to a list of nine "protected needs" (Defila and Di Giulio 2020); the park emerged as a unique satisfier for meeting multiple needs for diverse groups of people. In yet another study, Max-Neef's approach (see Box 2.2 and Annex 1) to human needs and satisfiers framed group discussions in Lleida, a medium-sized Catalonian city, revealing how social norms and local institutions can stifle needs satisfaction. In another study with the same methodology, researchers engaged with rural and urban communities in Medellín (Colombia) to better understand which energy services are necessary to satisfy human needs (Brand-Correa et al. 2018). Another series of needs-based workshops also adopted the Max-Neef approach to explore scenarios for sustainability with local stakeholders in a Belgian region (Jolibert et al. 2014).

(Continued)

These and other instances of transdisciplinary research document the ability of citizens, through participatory processes, to reach agreement on human needs and productively address questions of resource use and allocation.

Practice-driven participatory efforts are also underway in many places to gain a better understanding of the societal norms influencing perceived needs and wellbeing. One noteworthy example is the Minimum Living Standard (MLS) in the United Kingdom, which has highlighted the role of specific norms in influencing what people understand to be necessary. For example, a hair-straightening iron might be identified as a necessary appliance by some people in the United Kingdom by virtue of workplace expectations around hair styling (Walker et al. 2016). At a municipal level, there are also efforts underway to generate new indicators for wellbeing, emerging from citizen-led processes, such as the regional sustainable wellbeing indicators that emerged in the Grenoble area through citizen engagement (Les Indicators de Bien-être Soutenable Territorialisés – IBEST, from the Grenoble area, see Ottaviani 2018). Other processes are also underway that may not relate precisely to need satisfaction or tackle the question of wellbeing, but that nevertheless engage people in debating notions of limits, often within the context of the patterns of everyday life. Recognized examples in this context are the Transition Towns, the climate justice movement, climate citizen assemblies, Carbon Conversations, efforts underway in Social and Solidarity Economy (SSE) initiatives, and initiatives within the degrowth movement (Muraca and Döring 2018).

Getting started and building momentum

When it comes to social change and the transformation of society, almost anything is possible. Indeed, we have witnessed major change on many occasions. Take, for example, the 1926 Convention to Suppress the Slave Trade and Slavery, or the adoption of the Universal Declaration of Human Rights in 1948, with 48 member-states of the United Nations voting in support and 8 abstaining. Both were thought unlikely if not impossible prior to their passage. Or consider the civil rights movement in the United States, or the creation of the welfare state in Europe to combat the social costs of industrialization. Both led to changes, still unfolding, that many at the time thought to be idealistic or hopelessly naïve. These are a few of many examples of how societal change brings with it collective actions and alternative approaches that aim toward collective goals –what some call social innovation. If human ingenuity propelled such societal changes in the past, just imagine what people are capable of today, with the knowledge, expertise, and tools at hand. There is no reason why we, as a society, cannot imagine, plan, and achieve change for a more prosperous future.

Social change is not always incremental, linear, or tidy. It is typically messy business, rarely falling into neat conceptual boxes. People often talk about "bottom up" approaches that originate at the level of a community and trickle up to elite decision-makers, and "top down" initiatives that begin with elites and filter down to communities and individuals. Truthfully, change does not usually work this way. Openings and interventions for social change come from above, below, and across. They move in different directions and at different speeds, sometimes creating reinforcing feedback and other times working at cross-purposes. In today's networked world, a local initiative in Hungary to reduce energy consumption might spur a similar initiative in a Canadian neighborhood. A policy discussion around basic income in Switzerland might inspire similar efforts in Norway, Finland, or the United States.

Thus, when it comes to consumption corridors, no finalized, tested, or predictable strategy for change exists. We cannot know, today, what these corridors will look like, within different contexts and communities. And, if we are honest, we cannot know with certainty where a serious engagement with this corridors idea will take us. Will it mean that our lifestyles will have to dramatically change? Perhaps, but let's be clear on an essential point: this project is not about individuals taking on sole responsibility to limit their own consumption. It is about starting a conversation about what should be meaningful to us and our societies, including the global one, for a good life here and now, and in the future. Fundamentally, it is a discussion about needs and wellbeing at a collective level, rather than desires at an individual level.

Let us begin with introducing the idea of consumption corridors into society for discussion and debate. We can initiate conversations about consumption corridors within our families and peer groups, and with co-workers, neighbors, and others who share an interest in creating opportunities for a good life for all. What does it take for us to be able to live a good life? What is a good life as opposed to a better life?

We can also initiate these conversations in our communities, towns, or cities, and even take them to regional and national levels if we are equipped to do so. In these conversations, we might describe the idea of corridors and, importantly, reflect on how the conventional stories we tell ourselves about "solving" ecological and social sustainability challenges are misleading. By getting more and more people, and the organizations traditionally representing their interests, involved in the conversation, we can build momentum. We can begin to foster collective societal processes for pondering fundamental questions about our lives and our futures, which the consumption corridors concept invites us to ask.

There are other ways to influence societal pathways. We can write to politicians or organize petitions. We can exert pressure on provisioning systems via consumer groups. We can promote relevant deliberations and activities in our professional roles. We can work through our associations and networks to engage with consumption corridors and the good life. We can integrate these ideas into our teaching practice, or promote them in research agendas, as teachers and researchers respectively. Clearly, there are many avenues for exploring, with others, how our societies can live well within limits. Let us together take the needed steps toward imagining the future.

Note

1 https://www.unter1000.de/

4   What's stopping us?

Confronted by immense ecological and social challenges, it would make perfect sense to double-down on the tools and strategies that have produced significant improvement in the quality of life over the past decades: better technologies, for instance, or more efficiency, or stronger commitments to education. Won't those save us from having to pursue wellbeing *within limits*? The answer is an unequivocal "no."

It is surely true that technological innovation, efficiency, educated and responsible consumer behavior, and individual freedom all carry important benefits and are needed. But in their neglect of constraints and complexities, these dominant "solutions" and the claims they make about practicality and possibility discourage creative thinking about how to live well within limits–and in doing so, undermine the good life. Today's dominant stories about innovation, the market, and the role and power of consumers make it difficult to appreciate the need for fundamental social change. These narratives are just true enough to make them believable, and yet so deeply false as to make them dangerous.

All of which points to perhaps the most challenging requirement of good-life visioning: seeing clearly the limits of everyday stories about the wizardry of technology, the power of efficiency, the centrality of the consumer, and the role of freedom in democracy.

Limits to the salvation potential of technological innovation

Ask environmental policy specialists or environmental engineers about how best to save the planet, and most will respond with visions of exciting, even revolutionary technologies: renewable energy systems, hyper-efficient automobiles, green buildings, circular-economy industrial processes that eliminate waste, next-generation nuclear power, energy-intensive vertical farming to allow traditional farmland to return to the wild, and the like. Pose the same question to many development specialists and be prepared for much of the same: new agricultural technologies, infant rehydration packets, off-grid electrification systems, or cheap cell-phone technologies. The late anthropologist Clifford Geertz got it right when, more than 30 years ago, he observed that elite problem-solvers are happiest when they are talking about technological responses to knotty social issues.

It is no surprise, then, that many who are deeply concerned about environmental degradation and social injustice believe that society-saving technological innovations will arrive in time. They trust that these technologies are lurking just around the corner, ready to save the day if only we marshal sufficient imagination and boldness to deploy them. With some justification, these individuals sense that global systems of investment, innovation, and technological dissemination respond to business opportunities and government incentives, both of which are triggered by scarcity or crisis. They reason that when conditions get bad enough, innovations will come to market in response to mounting demand and willingness to pay. Consider, they say, the sudden shift to ozone-friendly refrigerants after the surprising discovery of the ozone hole in 1985, or today's rapid spread of solar panels and wind turbines in response to climate change. Crisis and the potential for profit heightens government support, corporate commitment, and consumer demand around new innovations – and technologists respond.

And really, why would one expect otherwise? After all, technological innovation – new artifacts, novel materials, pioneering techniques – has been the primary source of human prosperity. To deny this simple fact is to be churlish about the amazing creativity of the human species. Technological innovation defines the four great historical revolutions: agricultural, industrial, medical, and digital. It has made life better by liberating more resources, creating more opportunity, and opening up new possibilities. In many instances, innovations have produced large benefits for the masses at low cost, making it possible for writers like us to entertain the idea of a good life for all. Think of the positive impact of antibiotics on everyday life, for example, or of sanitary engineering or widespread electrification. All are powerful and liberating technologies.

This comforting story of technological innovation and historical salvation may help us sleep at night, but it is increasingly mismatched to current conditions in three dangerous ways, each inimical to the good life.

One centers on purchasing power and the further cementing of inequality. If technological innovation responds to consumer demand, then most new inventions will inevitably cater to the global affluent. Sadly, this dynamic of buying-power-driven innovation already prevails: more research and development dollars focus, for example, on new medications for the pets of the affluent than for all African tropical diseases. And monies spent on innovations in the packaging and distribution of bottled water for rich-world consumers dwarfs research and development investments in clean-water systems for the poor in Asia and Africa.

Exceptions exist, of course. A few global philanthropists apply their fortunes to health, sanitation, or environmental innovations for the poor, and inventors of cheap and resilient household water filters may find financial reward among the billions of people thirsting for clean water. But these are the exceptions that underscore the rule: innovation flows to where money is to be made – and in this increasingly unequal world, that money concentrates among a thin slice of humanity at the top.

In romanticizing the virtues of technological innovation, then, apostles of this story forget to ask about technological innovation *for whom*. Their view of innovation celebrates systems of investment and innovation that may address, in the short run, social and ecological problems, but that will almost surely widen the gap between the haves and have nots in the long run. Lost in a wave of technological optimism is a focus on who participates in deciding what innovations are developed, how they are implemented, and how these decisions affect the distribution of chances to live a good life.

A second danger of technological optimism flows from a reliance on faulty lessons from the past. Consider the challenge of the ozone hole mentioned above. In this often-cited instance, an environmental problem was rapidly addressed through the deft use of technology – in this case, refrigerants that are less hostile to stratospheric ozone. Major chemical industries came on board, countries banded together under the 1987 Montreal Protocol, and a major environmental and human-health disaster was averted. Many take this welcome success as proof, or at least compelling evidence, of the power of technological innovation.

Two details about this story are frequently lost, however, that should make us less sanguine about this power. One is that the "rescue technology" – alternatives to ozone-destroying CFCs – had already been developed in the 1970s in response to environmental concerns about propellants in spray cans. The other is that the commercial financial benefits from the deployment of these more expensive substitutes flowed largely to the same powerful actors (DuPont, in particular) that stood to lose the most from the phase-out of the offending refrigerants. Neither condition – planet-saving technologies already commercialized, and the focused distribution of costs and benefits on a single politically powerful actor, with the benefits dwarfing the costs – usually occurs, and both rarely do. That it happened around the ozone layer is good news, but treating these enabling conditions as the norm is a setup for self-delusion, and disaster for the good life.

Perhaps the greatest shortcoming of technological optimism, however, flows from a fundamental misunderstanding of environmental and social change. Stripped to its essentials, technological-salvation thinking, especially in its just-in-time form, is essentially reactive: a problem arises that is fixable, and new innovations come to life to fix it. But what if, as is true of so many environmental and social issues, the initial damages from the problem at hand are not easily reversed? Or, what if interactions among several seemingly manageable problems produce a challenge that is suddenly immediate and potentially catastrophic? There is little room for these scenarios in a just-in-time story of technological innovation, where the slow, linear escalation of problems provides technologists time to engineer solutions before time runs out. Yet many environmental and social problems are neither slow nor linear in their implications for human prosperity and the good life. The potential for sudden surprise and irreversible damage is all too real. These challenges demand an ethos not of technological cleverness, but of social prudence, of acting with humility and caution when confronted by risk and uncertainty. The French philosopher Hans Jonas calls this the "imperative of responsibility."

Indeed, if one believes only a fraction of what environmental scientists are saying about planetary boundaries and "safe operating space," then precaution is more prudent than hopeful faith in last-minute technological remedies. Many critical environmental and social systems appear near their breaking point. While the scientific community can point to looming dangers, it cannot speak with certainty about where the line in the sand is drawn. Even the natural scientists do not yet know enough about the intricacies of the nitrogen cycle, the reservoirs of disease that could be unleashed as biodiverse systems come under assault, or the complex feedbacks in our climate system to say just how much pollution or environmental degradation is acceptable. Additionally, and more important, they cannot with confidence predict how these systems interact under stress.

Against this backdrop of high-risk uncertainty, the good life is poorly served by technological thinking built on assumptions of problem linearity and reversibility. Yes, technological innovation has its place in any quest for the good life. But we now live in world of dramatic ecological and social challenges where placing hope in technology as a savior sets us up for disappointment and decline. We need social change based on prudence and precaution that complements the best innovations technologists can muster, and puts the right of individuals to pursue a good life front and center. And we need this change quickly.

Limits to efficiency and markets as solutions

A second dominant narrative focuses on the role of efficiency and markets as solutions to current ecological and social challenges. This narrative emphasizes the enormous potential for increasing the economic and technological efficiency of human activity, allowing humanity to squeeze more prosperity out of a lump of coal, a liter of water, a hectare of land, or an hour of time. And it concludes that reaching these efficiencies, often in cost-effective ways, will greatly diminish our shared environmental impact. This attractive "win-win" story, where rational resource use lightens our impact on the planet while fattening the pocketbooks of producers and consumers alike (thus incentivizing virtuous behaviors of efficiency and frugality) is almost too good to be true – because, almost always, it is.

One reason is faulty market signals. Innovations occur when the promise of profit exists, and possibilities for profit flow from the interplay of price and costs. When the social and environmental costs of production and consumption are externalized – that is, when these costs are not fully expressed in the price of the products we buy – the price of products that do harm are artificially low, and profits to be made from alternative products are subsequently depressed. This ubiquitous market failure, where prices fail to match real costs, produces patterns of innovation that pull us further away from solving pressing social problems. Think here, for example, of remarkable improvements in the fuel efficiency of aircraft, or massive cargo ships. These innovations facilitate more flying, and more individual consumption, and would have taken an entirely different form if the environmental and social costs of today's consumption were fully reflected in the prices we pay for products.

In addition, a relentless focus on efficiency does not produce absolute reductions in resource use over time. In many instances, increased efficiency leads to escalating consumption of the product at hand, swamping the environmental benefits from becoming more efficient in the first place. Examples abound. More efficient jet aircraft led to cheaper airfares, leading to more planes in air. Mandated efficiency improvements in refrigerators in Europe made these appliances less expensive to operate, facilitating a three-fold increase in the volume of refrigerators now on the market, with predictable impacts on electricity consumption. In other instances, increased efficiency produces more consumption of other products, with similar negative effects on the environment. Scientists call this dynamic the "rebound effect," and it is also known as the "Jevon's Paradox," named after the British economist who noted the rapid increase in coal consumption as the efficiency of steam engines increased (see Box 4.1: Why easy wins for more sustainable consumption won't be enough).

Numerous studies show these rebound effects to exist and to be substantial. Indeed, they are so significant that almost all of the gains that have been made with technological improvements in efficiency have been eaten up by increasing sizes, quantities, and levels of consumption. In the end, getting more efficient just means more growth. And this growth correlates with the use of more ecological resources rather than less. We now know that efficiency without a similarly robust focus on sufficiency – on "enoughness" and prudent restraint – will not save the day. Efficiency, without new forms of economic and social organization that slow the rate of growth and make it possible to prosper with less, cannot foster the good life.

It bears noting, finally, that patterns of inequity and injustice cannot be solved by improvements in technological efficiency. They are, in fact, often exacerbated, accidently or otherwise, by a single-minded preoccupation with producing and consuming more with less. Such was the lesson of "the gospel of efficiency" during the Progressive Era in the United States, which, as documented by historian Samuel P. Hayes, was a time of considerable concentration of economic and political power. More recently, examples from around the world demonstrate how initiatives to improve efficiency reduce the provision of services, fueling injustice and environmentally damaging behavior. In many European countries, for instance, railway services have been reduced for the sake of efficiency, exacerbating injustice in the mobility system while fostering increased reliance on auto and air travel. As environmental scholar Tom Princen calls out in his work on sufficiency, cooperation and compassion are too often at odds with the cold calculus of efficiency.

Surely, efficiency gains and well-functioning markets can support the pursuit of wellbeing within limits. In these efforts, however, commitments to efficiency must be paired with a focus on sufficiency and justice. Efficiency by itself is counter-productive when we forget, as is so often the case, that the main aim is to focus on what is really needed and how such needs can be met, with less, toward the aim of a good life for all.

Limits to consumer sovereignty and responsibility

The final narrative builds on the first two by offering a path for action. It is the familiar story about the imperative for individual consumers to "buy green" and "buy just," to purchase goods and services that reward environmentally and socially responsible innovation and support resource-efficient products and services. In this narrative, individual consumers have the ultimate power to drive economic and technological change for the better. Our consumer choices are sovereign – they are our own, they are powerful, and they will push competitive markets in the right direction.

The advent of a consumer sovereignty/individual control narrative parallels the re-emergence, in the early 1980s, of neo-liberalism, a political and social philosophy that emphasizes individual responsibility for larger social conditions. The rise of neo-liberalism, reflected in the policies of Ronald Reagan in the United States and Margaret Thatcher in the United Kingdom, was not the only force behind this narrative, however, and it may not have been the most important. Growing public concern about global environmental ills (punctuated by the utterly surprising and profoundly photogenic appearance of an "ozone hole" in 1985), declining corporate profits, and new pressures on mainstream environment groups interacted in unexpected ways to reinforce the then-new notion that consumer decisions could be among the most powerful forces for progressive social change (Maniates 2019). Since the insertion of this idea into mainstream public conversation in the late 1980s, the "consumers are king" story has grown more ubiquitous and entrenched.

The problem is not with "green" or "socially just" consumption per se. There are many good reasons to consume in ways that match our politics and reaffirm our social concerns: to enact and remind ourselves daily, in small ways, of our ethical responsibilities and planetary commitments; to support a treasured small business or artisan seeking to make the world better; to signal to others that we try, where we can, to walk our talk; to fit in with an esteemed social group; or to insulate ourselves from environmental harm (by, for example, buying organic foods or environmentally benign cleaning products or pest control).

Buying the "right" products to initiate fundamental social change does not rise to this list of "good reasons," simply because it does not work. This is in part because of an information problem – in particular, having the right information at the right time in an accessible way. Even the best-intentioned consumers do not have the time to gather and evaluate mountains of information about every consumption choice before them. Think of the proverbial small print on food products, using unintelligible language, but also the questionable validity of many of the nice-sounding labels, of which there are hundreds. And even if consumers have *all* the information they need, they often face a conundrum of having to choose between products that are either socially just or environmentally sound, but not always both. As a result, people often spend too much of their energy puzzling out the "right" choice that ends up having the most marginal of impacts, which fuels feelings of frustration and cynicism that can depress and disempower.

Even more fundamentally, every message directed at consumers about ecologically and socially superior consumption choices is overpowered by hundreds of messages persuading consumers to consume more. Even those messages with environmental or social content typically are messages enticing consumption. How often have you been asked to buy less? And it is not just the marketing departments of business actors at work here, but also governments and, unfortunately, some environmental groups.

The starkest danger of the "consumer in charge" narrative is that it depoliticizes the challenges before us, at a time when a citizen politics is most called for. With consumers in charge, only the softest and most benevolent policy interventions are required from governments, like providing consumers with information on the environmental and social characteristics of products, and information on how to use these products in a better (especially more efficient) way. For these reasons, the consumer sovereignty narrative is attractive to politicians, as it shifts responsibility away from producers, retailers, and those tasked with regulating commercial activity. In an attempt to move to a less confrontational politics of human flourishing in a world of ecological limits and social inequity (where one buys green and fair, and gently cajoles their friends and neighbors to do the same), we have landed in a depoliticized space, hoping that the diffusion of "good" consumer behavior from one consumer to another will coalesce into a wave of change.

But it cannot, for it assigns far too much responsibility to the individual consumer. Consumer demand can only exert a real impact on producers if two conditions obtain. One is the existence of genuine choice between "good" products and "bad." But, despite appearances, this is rarely the case; choices are packaged, curated, and obscured by adept marketers, who often hide the fact that the choice before consumers is between two "bad" products, one marginally less so than the other. Another is strategic coordination: a great many consumers must make the same product choices at the same time, with persistence. But this requires a level of diligence, focus, conviction, and resistance to greenwashing that does not emerge spontaneously. It comes from collective action, most often promoted and organized by civil society organizations.

The need for such collective action is made all the more necessary by the prevalence of individual and collective routines and practices. People cannot reason and weigh every consumer decision every time they act. Most of the hundreds of small decisions we make are based on daily routines. We simply would not be able to function otherwise. And our routines, in turn, are strongly influenced by their social and material contexts. Time, societal norms of comfort and appropriate behavior, and financial structures, all play a role here. Breaking routines and practices requires far more than the provision of information about products and product use. It requires a change in the institutions and structures supporting them.

There is broad consensus among sustainable consumption scholars that well-meaning individuals, left to their own convictions, will make inferior and insufficiently persistent consumption choices when it comes to sustainability and social-justice characteristics. Prevailing

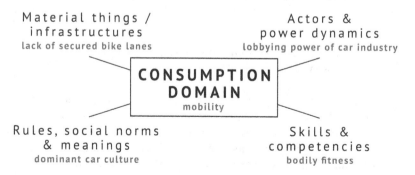

Figure 4.1 Socio-material mapping of satisfiers.

routines and practices, and information and time constraints amplified by subtle (and sometimes not so subtle) manipulations by producers, retailers, and marketers are too strong a barrier to overcome. The result is a pronounced attitude-behavior gap (see Box 4.1: Why easy wins for more sustainable consumption won't be enough) that leaves unchallenged the primary threats to a good life for all.

For all these reasons, the sovereign consumer narrative is dangerous because it reduces individuals to their role as consumers, and blames them for social ills that allegedly arise from "poor" consumption choices. The resulting focus on saving the world as a consumer, one green-lifestyle action at a time, blocks inspirational avenues to working collectively as citizens toward the good life. It damages our political imaginaries around our possible roles as citizens. At a moment in human history when what we most need are sources of and strategies for social change that cultivate prudence and precaution, we instead get short lists of how to save the world one conscientious purchase at a time.

This must change. The voting-with-your-purchases narrative, although constructed for us, has found fertile ground because of the combination of (a) a growing sense of urgency among many that something must be done about the environment, and (b) a deepening confusion about how one productively engages in "politics" and "structural change." Together, (a) + (b) enable the prevailing story that the checkout line at the market is where we can do the most good for the planet, and for those treated unjustly. Recent developments indicate that individuals and groups are increasingly challenging this story, however. Fridays for Future, Extinction Rebellion, and other initiatives are once again making environmental and social policy a question of political engagement. Let us join them in re-appreciating and regaining our political power and capacities.

Box 4.1: Why easy wins for more sustainable consumption won't be enough

Sustainable consumption scholars offer several explanations for why earth-friendly, justice-supporting consumers falter when it comes to translating their values into meaningful impact. One reason is "information asymmetries" between producers and consumers – in other words, producers up and down the supply chain can hide the negative social and environmental impacts of their operations, putting conscientious consumers at a disadvantage. This is what Princen (1997) calls "the shading and distancing of commerce," a key element in the systematic separation of production practices from consumption decisions. Another is the outsized role of time constraints, competing values, and everyday routines, which together thwart the rational intentions of well-meaning consumers (Røpke 1999). These factors, and others like them, suggest that assigning primary responsibility for system change to individual consumers is anathema to transformative change (Maniates 2001, 2019).

Three dynamics are especially illustrative of the constraints and disappointments that inevitably arise when one seeks sustainability transformation via greater technological efficiency, more enlightened consumer action, or both:

(a) Rebound effects

More efficient technologies are thought to be one easy way to address unsustainable consumption patterns. However, a rebound effect occurs when efficiency improvements produce increased consumption. This occurs via "direct rebound," when consumption around the good experiencing the efficiency improvement increases (for example, driving a fuel-efficient car more than a petrol-guzzler), or through "indirect rebound," when money saved from efficiencies from one product is spent elsewhere (for example, buying a larger home with more furniture because of lower electricity bills from energy-efficiency improvements). Empirical studies demonstrate how increases in consumption consistently thwart efficiency-driven resource savings across a wide variety of sectors (Stern 2020). This is why sustainability scholars increasingly critique "efficiency" both as a concept (Shove 2018) and as a form of "weak sustainable consumption governance" (Fuchs and Lorek 2005). Many argue that, to be successful, efficiency measures must be accompanied by initiatives that limit overall levels of consumption, that is, "strong sustainable consumption governance."

(b) Attitude-behavior gap

Altering consumer attitudes, often through information campaigns or incentives, was thought to be another straightforward

(Continued)

way of fostering environmental sustainability while preserving chances for the good life. But this approach has foundered on the rocks of the so-called attitude-behavior (or value-action) gap (Flynn et al. 2009, Kollmuss and Agyeman 2002). This gap describes the failure of growing consumer concern for the environment to translate into meaningful behavior change. This divide between attitudes and action suggests the presence of other, often more powerful forces on consumption choices. These include convenience, financial concerns, status and identity considerations, and "lock in" effects. Lock-in effects, also known as "path dependencies," describe the power of existing infrastructures and norms over consumer choice. People, for instance, can become locked into automobile usage because of existing auto-centric infrastructures and technologies, or because of social norms and collective conventions around mobility (Sahakian 2017). The notion that attitudes influence behaviors and choices is thus an oversimplistic understanding of how social change comes about (Shove 2010).

(c) Behavior-impact gap

Policymakers, academics, and environmental organizations long thought that steering conscientious consumers toward ecologically or socially superior consumption choices – often via labeling, social media, or environmental- or carbon-footprint calculators – could foster important environmental improvements. The so-called behavior-impact gap says otherwise. Strikingly, consumers who intentionally pursue environmentally superior consumption choices find it difficult to meaningfully shrink their ecological footprint. One influential, frequently cited study (Csutora 2012) notes that differences in the ecological footprints of "green" and "brown consumers" are often insignificant and cannot drive reductions in resource consumption needed for long-term sustainability. A more recent analysis (Moser and Kleinhückelkotten 2018) reaches much the same conclusion, underscoring the primary effect of income, rather than consumer intentionality, on one's overall ecological footprint. Likewise, a study on food consumption in Switzerland found that the environmental impact of vegan and vegetarian diets was much lower than that of meat-based diets, but still above 0.6 ton CO_2 / per year – this because of the general carbon intensity of food production and distribution systems (Ernstoff et al. 2020). This suggests that making environmentally (or socially) superior consumption choices usually is not enough. Institutional arrangements, infrastructures, and collective conventions must also change.

These three phenomena – rebound effects, attitude-behavior gaps, and behavior-impact gaps – capture powerful dynamics that contribute to the failure of technological innovation, efficiency, and consumer sovereignty as saviors. They underscore how we delude ourselves with the stories described in this chapter. In the end, with all the technological innovation we have achieved, with markets forcefully pushing for efficiency, and with persistent efforts to educate consumers, we are far from a decoupling of material consumption from resource use (Jackson 2017, Wiedmann et al. 2020). As long as problems are framed as a function of inefficient technologies or bad individual choices, we will keep returning to the same tired solutions, to the detriment of bolder possibilities for necessary system change.

No limits to freedom in democratic societies?

As we push forward toward living well within limits through consumption corridors, objections will surely arise. These objections rarely sprout from malice; misunderstanding, uncertainty, and fear are more typical sources. After all, any change has winners and losers, and when presented with the notion of consumption corridors, some may perceive themselves, or their family and friends, as losing under corridor arrangements.

One major objection to consumption corridors is that they will restrict individual freedom, a core value in liberal democracies. Nobody, under this argument, has the right to constrain individual consumption choices or limit one's overall consumption. This argument reflects a sense of entitlement as well as the inclination to put individual freedom first.

In many modern societies, freedom is a highly treasured value and frequently referenced in arguments that all individuals should be as free as possible in their decisions and actions. And yes, it would be utterly wrong to question the importance of freedom. Ideas of freedom of speech, freedom of conscience, freedom of religious belief and expression, and freedom of economic exchange, among others, all follow from historically inspired efforts to establish protected spaces as guarantees against despotism – and quite often, freedom is a hard-won thing. It is therefore understandable that freedom came to be a central value in liberal democratic societies.

Yet, political claims for the utmost freedom forget that freedom can only be guaranteed by the simultaneous exercise of necessary constraints. Liberal democratic societies do not choose between the expansion of freedom and the setting of limits, but pursue both. Freedom and limits are not separate political projects that can be differentiated according to party lines. On the contrary, the development of individual freedoms and the limits to keep collective freedoms intact evolve mutually, similar to the creation of safe and secure spaces for people to live in while simultaneously allowing for human differences and creativity.

In this way, limits secure and enhance freedom. Indeed, freedom and limits are mutually supportive, and societal as well as individual conceptions of the good life flourish not despite, but because of the existence of limits. Accordingly, democratic states have always limited the freedom of citizens for the pursuit of security and the safeguarding of its citizens. Freedom is not only relevant in terms of "freedom from" (specifically interventions in my freedom by the state or society), but also "freedom to" (such as to engage in religious practices).

Of course, a tension will always exist between individual freedom and the authority of the state to protect other individuals and society as a whole. This tension was visible when public-health limits on individual freedom to gather, travel, or work were imposed during the COVID-19 pandemic, and fiercely debated and contested in some sectors of societies. Indeed, all of the freedoms listed above exhibit this tension. While people must be free to do certain things, they also must be free from certain threats, especially threats from the exercise of the freedom of others. Doing whatever you like just might not be good for everyone around you. This is especially true in a socially and ecologically exploited world, where the goal of living well within limits, and questions of justice and responsibility, deeply converge.

It is the very notion of individuals living together in societies, and creating and using the state to govern society in the pursuit of the common good, that supports the rule that the freedom of the individual must be limited when it impinges on the wellbeing of others. This idea is embodied, for instance, in §2 of the German Basic Law (Grundgesetz): "Every person shall have the right to free development of his personality insofar as he does not violate the rights of others."

The task of society and the state is to carefully weigh the guarantee of individual freedom against the desire to foster the wellbeing of society and the protection of the weak and vulnerable. Constraints on individual freedom should not be imposed too freely. But if the individual and/or society as a whole requires protection from damage inflicted by other individuals or groups in that society, the state has the obligation to impose limits on individual behavior. Consequently, the idea of imposing constraints on consumption choices should not appear as a challenge to general societal practice, especially when certain forms of human consumption are fostering social exploitation and challenging planetary boundaries.

Taking a different perspective, we may consider self-chosen limits as expressions of freedom. Exercising restraint by imposing rules upon ourselves is the very essence of autonomy. Viewed this way, the innovative potential of limits becomes visible. Limits can be a powerful creative element, not only in an abstract sense, but also in everyday practices and choices.

Often people feel they must sacrifice elements of their current lifestyle in order to make limits work, or they may feel that limits are imposed on them, be it by governments, employers, or others. However, if as individuals and societies, we limit ourselves willingly in pursuit of a larger goal, the imposition of such limits becomes an act of freedom. Limits become a conscious choice to go for something we care about more. That is why such limits should be something we develop through a participatory process. Giving up highly materialistic, overworked and stressed lifestyles, for instance, can be experienced by individuals as freedom to live more authentic lives. Similarly, ecological risks threaten the forced imposition of limits on societies in the future, while more sustainable, less consumerist lifestyles can be an expression of and contribution to freedom, now and for generations to come.

Self-chosen limits set people free. If, as individuals and societies, we can choose to live within limits, a democratic transition to a more sustainable world is possible.

Shedding myths in pursuit of social change

The power of the stories we tell about technological innovation, efficiency, consumer sovereignty, and individual freedom is formidable. This is not surprising. These stories are familiar, comforting, often hopeful, grounded in familiar truths, and thus deeply alluring. They appeal to a human fascination with the novel, the shiny, the creative and clever. Because they validate familiar structures of investment, production, and consumption, these stories reaffirm settled world views and seem to demand little in terms of upsetting change. Importantly, they offer respite from prolonged conflict over complex social problems, either by creating "everyone wins, no one loses" or "just deal with it, you can't fight progress" solutions. This framing holds special sway over policymakers and other elites who seek to avoid political controversy and public discontent. No one with a crystal ball need be responsible for planning or advancing innovation. Instead, innovation just happens and diffuses, on its own when the time is right, through Adam Smith's hidden hand of the marketplace. Informed and conscientious consumers can nudge innovation along by buying green or consuming in socially responsible ways. And the aggregate result of freely chosen values and actions by reasonable individuals will be a better future for all.

These framings imperil the good life. Preoccupation with new gadgets and nifty tools, efficiency promises and smart consumer choice, and unlimited freedom and entitlement erodes our ability to address fundamental issues of justice and power, and to imagine workable paths to a better future. This preoccupation has no place in any credible, compelling vision for the pursuit of a good life – not because notions of the good life are anti-technological, anti-market, or anti-freedom, but because society's sometimes cultish obsession with new artifacts, innovative production-processes, and narratives of consumer sovereignty and individual control undermines our capacity to recognize the need for social change and inhibits our ability to pursue it.

More than ever before, these stories reveal how we have become locked into debilitating material and social structures. As guideposts to action they are out of sync with needed transformative change. Enacting these stories creates a false sense of progress and robs us of our remarkable human ability to resolve complex problems. *Changing times* demand social change, without relying on the mythical autonomous interplay of market and technology in our pursuit of the good life. We need social change that facilitates rewarding, affirming, and meaningful citizen participation instead of consumer choice. Consumption corridors offer just that opportunity.

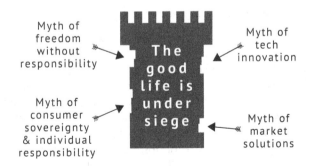

Figure 4.2 What's stopping us.

5 Visionary change

Corridors as a pathway to the good life

The good life. Human flourishing. Rights and responsibilities, needs and satisfiers, planetary limits and gross inequality. And, of course, consumption corridors and the participatory processes they require and inspire. These concepts, explicated over the past chapters, are important tools for understanding and acting upon the world. Underlying them all – or, rather, underlying how this book knits these elements together – is a singular assertion, possibly offensive to some while commonsensical to others: when it comes to consumption choices that go beyond meeting needs, humans are not always smart. Acting as consumers, disconnected from searching and sometimes difficult conversations about what it means to live a good life, people may behave in ways contrary to their deepest aspirations and most cherished beliefs, making the good life exceedingly difficult to achieve.

The problem, hinted at in prior chapters, is the convoluted interplay among the *material need* to consume, the *cultural and psychological* significance of consumption choices in daily life, and the *power of stories and of those who shape them*. Sitting alone on a desert island, drinking milk from a coconut, is a simple act of satisfying one's need for nourishment. But within a community, the coconut and its milk can become much more: a signal to other coconut-milk gourmands that you belong, a play for status among colleagues who favor more pedestrian beverages, a real bargain when harvested from your own tree, a statement of support for coconut rights, or a fear-of-missing-out choice seeded by savvy marketers. Once human needs are met, such as nourishment, physical safety, affection, or participation – consumption choices become interestingly complicated, and not always for the best.

Consider housing, the focus of Box 3.3 a few pages back. Over the past few decades, average home size around the world has increased dramatically. While some good has surely come from this, studies of the growing prominence of "McMansions"– extra-large homes built *en masse* at great environmental cost – reveal two unsettling patterns. One is rising discontent among owners of normal-sized homes when a flock of McMansions perches nearby, or when a co-worker or friend makes the jump to McMansion Land. The other is the lack of enduring satisfaction among those who upscale to McMansions – indeed, researchers frequently observe a decline in contentment, perhaps as the demands related to maintaining larger homes become slowly evident to their owners.

Both patterns are explained by the propensity of humans, social animals to the core, to compare their consumption to that of others, and to derive pain or pleasure from feelings of missing out or leading the pack. It is no surprise, then, that owners of normal homes can feel diminished when faced with "better" housing owned by people thought to be contemporaries. What was satisfyingly sufficient, or even more than enough, suddenly feels stingingly inadequate, especially as McMansions become reframed by certain builders and media channels as the new normal, the accepted sign of success, and the natural evolution of "necessary" housing – all standard tricks of a huge marketing industry.

Of course, new owners of McMansions don't enjoy immunity from these dynamics by virtue of their expansive domiciles. Once the flush of accomplishment from upscaling dissipates (and it quickly does), they adopt fellow McMansion owners as their new comparison group, and thus once again become just one of the crowd – nothing special, nothing distinctive, no special status. And the cycle begins anew: McMansion owners with sufficient financial power or capacity to borrow set their sights on even larger, custom-built estates in an attempt to catch up with colleagues or friends who have departed McMansion-land for even more opulent pastures. The result, as noted in Box 3.3: home sizes go up, the consumption of energy and other consumables needed to condition and outfit these new homes increases, and the planet groans under the weight, all with no apparent increase in overall quality of life.

Housing is but one example of this ubiquitous dynamic, which benefits from easy consumer credit, choice-editing by distributors and marketing specialists that supplants meaningful choice with managed behavior, and dominant narratives of shared prosperity via individual acquisition. The ensuing no-win treadmill of wants morphing into perceived needs, to be supplanted by even more ambitious wants, is anathema to the good life. No one becomes better off when consumption becomes a comparative performance on a continuously rising floor. And preaching at people to halt their needless upscaling, though momentarily satisfying, provides no escape from this dysfunction. It arises from collective social forces, from humans living within webs of inequality and political power, and it must be tackled at that level, through structural change, leavened by collective conversation and debate.

This book champions such a strategy of structural change, one that understands people as members of communities that must flourish within limits if all individuals are to find their way. In this approach, the promise of the good life for all, which highlights collective rights and responsibilities and valorizes ethically defensible ways of living, lights the way. The adventurous and collaborative design of consumption corridors becomes the process for organizing and implementing these principles, where everyone will be free to design a good life in the space between consumption minima and maxima.

This vision will seem utopian to some. If it didn't, this book would have aimed too low. Recent social upheaval together with the study of past moments of cultural transformation makes one fact clear, however: fundamental shifts toward new ways of thinking and acting do not happen through appeals to individual wellbeing. Structural racism is not effectively challenged and overcome, for instance, by appealing to white people's personal sense of prosperity or security. The level of change demanded by the promise of the good life and the pressures deriving from social inequities and ecological challenges requires a searching rethink of how we understand and organize our consumption practices and systems.

And, truly, beginning this work should not be a hard sell. Every major religion speaks to the essential intertwining of human restraint, personal wellbeing, and community vitality, as do areligious analogs like secular humanism and organized atheism. In the Christian faith, readers of the King James version of the Bible will recognize "when there is no vision, the people will perish" as the beginning of Proverbs 29:18, a call to Christian ideals of justice, restraint, and loving one's neighbor. But Christianity enjoys no monopoly on this vision, of course.

This vision thrives in these early decades of the 21st century. People are generally good. They care for family members, engage in community events, and help their neighbors. They labor to piece together a materially viable, socially generous, and morally uplifting life under frequently difficult circumstances. They do not always succeed, and when they stumble, they usually know. This book stands on that conviction, on the belief that a deep well of yearning for a better world exists, waiting to be facilitated in service of needed social change.

But what kind of change, and how? If you come from the mainstream of environmental problem-solving or social-policy analysis, you likely frame change in relation to individual actions ("get people to drive less") or technological change ("more wind power"), with the focus on individual consumer action in support of technological innovation. This species of change remains necessary but is no longer sufficient. Needed now are new kinds of social innovations that foster commitments to community within terrains of inequality and ecological decline, and infuse everyday life with a deep desire to build, with others, a genuinely sustainable future.

Consumption corridors offer a pathway to these changes. They envision a positive future of the good life for all. They articulate and propagate justice, elevate mindfulness about wants versus needs, and preserve freedom within limits in ways that mirror everyday strategies of satisfied and responsible people who know they cannot have it all. By their very nature, consumption corridors foster and facilitate engaged citizenship, and pull humanity back from planetary limits and social exploitation.

Two elements of consumption corridors emerge here as especially important. First, they are socially and culturally spacious, respecting diversity at a moment where one-size-fits-all responses to global ills are counterproductive. By defining minimum consumption standards (providing the basis for a good life to an individual) and maximum consumption standards (ensuring that one individual's consumption does not imperil other individuals' abilities to achieve minimum consumption standards in a world of limited resources), corridors create room for individual notions of a good life, allowing everyone a fulfilling life according to their own preferences.

Second, and most fundamentally, consumption corridors steer away from politically toxic calls for sacrifice as determined by distant experts or special interests. By tying the question of limits to human needs and requirements for their satisfaction, they neither demand asceticism or renunciation, nor pursue unspecified moral suasion in terms of "we should consume less." Rather, they highlight the necessity – difficult to pursue but rich in participatory rewards – to jointly define the conditions necessary to live a good life, and the subsequent steps necessary to make such a good life possible for all individuals. By providing freedom to pursue the good life in an ecologically and socially frayed world, these limits offer the benefit of ensuring that all other individuals living now and into the future can do so as well.

Humans are creative creatures. They are good at building powerfully impressive realities out of little more than imagined possibility. Around the world, the growing visibility of right-wing politics, structural racism, social inequality, and climate change is generating community- and city-level engagement, town hall meetings, peaceful protests, greater citizen involvement, and social online movements that push back, that seek another way. Many people are angry and indignant; many more know that something is not working and that some form of change is needed. Let us take this energy and mobilize it in pursuit of positive goals. Let us imagine, design, and implement new ways of living and thriving, properly connected to what we love, respect, and cherish in our own lives. To rescue the good life for all.

Annex 1: Needs

Below, we provide four lists of human needs, suggested by different scholars, that are used in sustainability research. Examining the needs named in these lists may provide readers with a better image of what a needs-based focus is about. The lists differ in terms of the names and number of needs identified, and the reasoning identification underlying their selection. In each case, relevant publications are cited so that those interested can easily access further information.

Based on: Max-Neef, M. A. (1991). *Human Scale Development Conception Application and Further Reflections.* **London: Apex Press.**

	Being	*Having*	*Doing*	*Interacting*
Subsistence				
Protection				
Affection				
Understanding				
Participation				
Idleness				
Creation				
Identity				
Freedom				

**Based on: Costanza, R., et al. (2007). Quality of Life: An
Approach Integrating Opportunities, Human Needs, and
Subjective Well-being.** *Ecological Economics* **61: 267–276.**

Human needs	Descriptors (direct satisfiers)
Subsistence	Food, shelter, vital ecological services (clean air and water, etc.) healthcare, rest
Reproduction	Nurturing of children, pregnant women Transmission of the culture Homemaking
Security	Enforced predictable rules of conduct Safety from violence at home and in public Security of subsistence into the future Maintain safe distance from crossing critical ecological thresholds Stewardship of nature to ensure subsistence into the future Care for the sick and elderly
Affection	"Being able to have attachments to things and persons outside ourselves; to love those who love and care for us, to grieve at their absence." (Nussbaum) Solidarity, respect, tolerance, generosity, passion, receptiveness
Understanding	Access to information Intuition and rationality
Participation	To act meaningfully in the world Contribute to and have some control over political, community, and social life Being heard Meaningful employment Citizenship
Leisure	Recreation, relaxation, tranquility, access to nature, travel
Spirituality	Engaging in transcendent experiences Access to nature Participation in a community of faith
Creativity/ emotional expression	Play, imagination, inventiveness, artistic expression
Identity	Status, recognition, sense of belonging, differentiation, sense of place
Freedom	"Being able to live one's own life and nobody else's. This means having certain guarantees of non-interference with certain choices that are especially personal and definitive of selfhood, such as choices regarding marriage, childbearing, sexual expression, speech and employment" (Nussbaum) Mobility

Based on: Di Giulio, A. and Defila, R. 2020. The 'Good Life' and Protected Needs. In: Kalfagianni, A., Fuchs, D. and Hayden, A. (eds.). *The Routledge Handbook of Global Sustainability Governance.* **London: Routledge.**

Group 1, focusing upon tangibles, material things (Protected Needs 1–3)

Need (what individuals must be allowed to want)	*Specified description: Individuals should have the possibility…*
1 To be provided with the material necessities for life	… to feed themselves sufficiently, with variety, and with food that is not detrimental to health.
	… to live in a suitably protected and equipped accommodation, offering privacy and sufficient space and allowing them to realise their idea of living.
	… to care for their bodies with dignity and dress suitably.
2 To realize their own conception of daily life	… to shape their daily life according to their own ideas.
	… to procure and use the material necessities for life from a diverse range of supply, and to have sufficient means to do so.
	… to move freely in public space.
3 To live in a livable environment	… to live in an environment (built and natural) that is not harmful to health and is aesthetically pleasing.
	… to develop a sensorial and emotional relationship with nature.
	… to have access to and be able to move about in diverse natural and cultural landscapes.

Group 2, focusing upon the person (Protected Needs 4–6)

Need (what individuals must be allowed to want)	*Specified description: Individuals should have the possibility…*
4 To develop as a person	… to develop their potential (knowledge, skills, attitudes, feelings, etc.) and thus their individual identity.
	… to face the challenges of their choice.
	… to freely access reliable information and thus form their own opinion.
5 To make their own life choices	… to freely decide and act upon the value-orientations they choose to adopt or reject (spirituality, religiosity, ideology, etc.).
	… to set their own life goals and pursue them.
	… to determine how they want to lead their life in terms of intimate relationships, family planning, where to live, etc.

(Continued)

Group 2, focusing upon the person (Protected Needs 4–6)

6 To perform activities valuable to them	… to carry out activities that they consider to be fulfilling (in work and leisure; paid and unpaid).
	… to carry out activities that match their personality and in which they can unfold their potential (in work and leisure; paid and unpaid).
	… to allocate their time for their different activities according to their own preferences and to have time for idleness.

Group 3, focusing upon community (Protected Needs 7–9)

Need (what individuals must be allowed to want)	Specified description: Individuals should have the possibility…
7 To be part of a community	… to maintain social relationships with other people (private, professional, during training, etc.).
	… to take part in cultural activities and celebrations and to participate in associations.
	… to access the cultural and historical heritage of their community.
8 To have a say in the shaping of society	… to co-determine the affairs of the society in which they live.
	… to take an active stand for concerns and problems (local, national, international) they hold dear.
	… to voice their opinion, by themselves and with others.
9 To be granted protection by society	… to be protected from public and private violence, from infringements on physical and mental integrity, and from natural hazards.
	… to pursue their goals without discrimination and with equal opportunity, to live in legal certainty, and to be treated with dignity and respect.
	… to be supported in the event of physical or mental impairment, unemployment, poverty, and other impairing conditions.

Based on: Doyal, L. and Gough, I. 1991. *A Theory of Human Need.* **Basingstoke: Macmillan.**

The following list of needs, originally developed by Doyal and Gough in 1991, is re-interpreted here by Julia K. Steinberger, University of Lausanne: "Well-being theorists Len Doyal and Ian Gough present a compelling picture of human need satisfaction: we all share a finite number of satiable and non-substitutable human needs. According to them, well-being can be understood roughly as a pyramid, with basic need satisfaction at the bottom underpinning physical, mental health and autonomy, culminating in well-being and social participation." – JKS

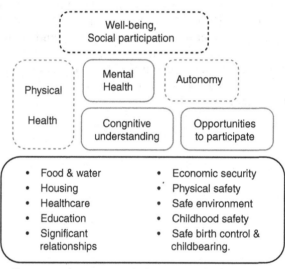

Source: https://www.opendemocracy.net/en/oureconomy/pandenomics-story-life-versus-growth/ (based on Goyal and Dough 1991)

Annex 2: Indicators of quality of life

Numerous indicators and indexes exist that attempt to measure (aspects of) wellbeing and quality of life. The table below lists relevant international efforts to develop indicators that broadly assess quality of life as a function of human wellbeing and environmental sustainability. (For additional information on the development of quality-of-life indices, see Fuchs et al. 2020.) To facilitate useful comparison, only those indicator sets covering at least 30 countries and multiple time points are included here.

Indicator set	Type	Institutional source	Countries covered (No.)	Years covered
BTI	Composite index	Bertelsmann Foundation	129	2006, 2008, 2010, 2012, 2014, 2016, 2018 (ongoing)
EPI	Composite index	Yale University	180	2006, 2008, 2010, 2012, 2014, 2016, 2018 (ongoing)
GS (adjusted net savings)	Adjusted national accounts	World Bank	141	1990–2017 (ongoing)
HPI	Composite index	The New Economics Foundation	161	2006, 2009, 2012, 2016 (ongoing)
HDI	Composite index	UNDP	189	1990–2017 (ongoing)
IIAG	Composite index	Mo Ibrahim Foundation	54	2008–2017 (ongoing)
IWI	Adjusted national accounts	UN; United Nations University; Int. Human Dimensions Programme on Global Environmental Change; UNEP; UNESCO	140	1990–2014 (ongoing)
BLI	Composite index	OECD	36	2011–2017 (ongoing)
SSI	Composite index	Sustainable Society Foundation	154	2006, 2008, 2010, 2012, 2014, 2016 (ongoing)

Data for countries covered relate to the most recent version of each indicator set (earlier versions may cover fewer countries). Data for years covered relate to the situation in March 2020.
Source: Fuchs et al. 2020.

Annex 3: Estimates of upper and lower sustainable limits in floor space

	Estimated minimum standard		Estimated maximum standard	
Household Size	Single household	4-person household	Single household	4-person household
Lower estimate	13,9 m²*	40 m²**	20 m²***	80 m²***
Higher estimate	30 m²**	41,8 m²*	30 m²****	120 m²****

* (Cohen 2020); ** (Rao and Min 2018); *** (Lettenmeier 2018); **** (Grubler et al. 2018), cited from Lorek and Spangenberg 2019.

References

Abramovitz, M. 1959. The Welfare Interpretation of Secular Trends in National Income and Product. In: Abramovitz, M., et al. (eds.). *The Allocation of Economic Resources*. Stanford, CA: Stanford University Press, 1–22.

Anand, S. and Sen, A. 1994. Sustainable Human Development: Concepts and Priorities. UNDP Human Development Report Office 1994 Occasional Papers. Available at SSRN: https://papers.ssrn.com/sol3/papers.cfm?abstract_id=2294664.

Banerjee, A. and Duflo, E. 2011. *Poor Economics: A Radical Rethinking of the Way to Fight Global Poverty*. New York: Public Affairs.

Bierwirth, A. and Thomas, S. 2019. Estimating the Sufficiency Potential in Buildings: The Space between Underdimensioned and Oversized. *ECEEE Summer Study Proceedings* 2019: 1143–1153.

Blättel-Mink, B., Brohmann, B., Defila, R., Di Giulio, A., Fischer, D., Fuchs, D., Gölz, S., Götz, K., Homburg, A., Kaufmann-Hayoz, R., Matthies, E., Michelsen, G., Schäfer, M., Tews, K., Wassermann, S. and Zundel. S. 2013. *Konsum-Botschaften: Was Forschende für die gesellschaftliche Gestaltung nachhaltigen Konsums empfehlen*. Stuttgart: Hirzel.

Brand-Correa, L., Martin-Ortega, J. and Steinberger, J. 2018. Human Scale Energy Services: Untangling a 'Golden Thread'. *Energy Research and Social Sciences* 38: 178–187.

Brand-Correa, L. and Steinberger, J. 2017. A Framework for Decoupling Human Need Satisfaction from Energy Use. *Ecological Economics* 141: 43–52.

Cohen, M. 2020. New Conceptions of Sufficient Home Size in High-Income Countries: Are We Approaching a Sustainable Consumption Transition? *Housing Theory and Society*. doi:10.1080/14036096.2020.1722218.

Coote, A. and Percy, A. 2020. *The Case for Universal Basic Services*. Cambridge: Polity Press.

Costanza, R., Fisher, B., Ali, S., Beer, C., Bond, L., Boumans, R., Danigelis, N. L., Dickinson, J., Elliott, C., Farley, J., Elliott Gayer, D., MacDonald, G. L., Hudspeth, T., Mahoney, D., McCahil, L., McIntosh, B., Reed, B., Turab Rizvi, S. A., Rizzo, D. M., Simpatico, T. and Snapp, R. 2007. Quality of Life: An Approach Integrating Opportunities, Human Needs, and Subjective Wellbeing. *Ecological Economics* 61: 267–276.

Costanza, R., Kubiszewski, I., Giovannini, E., Lovins, H., McGlade, J., Pickett, K. E., Ragnarsdóttir, K. V., Roberts, D., De Vogli, R. and Wilkinson, R. 2014. Time to Leave GDP Behind – Comment. *Nature* 505: 283–285.

Csutora, M. 2012. One More Awareness Gap? The Behavior-impact Gap Problem. *Journal of Consumer Policy* 35: 145–163.

Dearing, J., Wang, R., Zhang, K., Dyke, J. G., Haberl, H., Hossain, S. Md., Langdon, P. G., Lenton, T. M., Raworth, K., Brown, S., Carstensen, J., Cole, M. J., Cornell, S. E., Dawson, T. P., Doncaster, C. P., Eigenbrod, F., Flörke, M., Jeffers, E., Mackay, A. W., Nykvistk, B. and Poppy, G. M. 2014. Safe and Just Operating Spaces for Regional Social-ecological Systems. *Global Environmental Change* 28: 227–238. doi.org/10.1016/j.gloenvcha.2014.06.012.

Defila, R. and Di Giulio, A. 2020. The Concept of "Consumption Corridors" Meets Society – How an Idea for Fundamental Changes in Consumption is Received. *Journal of Consumer Policy* 43: 315–344. doi:10.1007/s10603-019-09437-w

Di Giulio, A. and Defila, R. 2020. The 'Good Life' and Protected Needs. In: Kalfagianni, A., Fuchs D. and Hayden, A. (eds.). *The Routledge Handbook of Global Sustainability Governance*. London: Routledge, 100–114.

Di Giulio, A. and Fuchs, D. 2014. Sustainable Consumption Corridors: Concept, Objections, and Responses. *GAIA* 23(1): 184–192.

Doyal, L. and Gough, I. 1991. *A Theory of Human Need*. Basingstoke: Macmillan.

Ernstoff, A., Stylianou, K., Sahakian, M., Godin, L., Dauriat, A., Humbert, S., Erkman, S. and Jolliet, O. 2020. Towards Win–Win Policies for Healthy and Sustainable Diets in Switzerland. *Nutrients* 12(275): 1–24.

Fleurbaey, M. and Blanchet, D. 2013. *Beyond GDP: Measuring Welfare and Assessing Sustainability*. Oxford: Oxford University Press.

Flynn, R., Bellaby, P. and Ricci, M. 2009. The "Value-action Gap" in Public Attitudes towards Sustainable Energy: The Case of Hydrogen Energy. *The Sociological Review* 57(2): 159–180. doi.org/10.1111/j.1467-954X.2010.01891.x.

Frank, R. 2000. *Luxury Fever: Money and Happiness in an Era of Excess*. Princeton, NJ: Princeton University Press.

Fuchs, D. 2020. Living Well within Limits: The Vision of Consumption Corridors. In: Kalfagianni, A., Fuchs, D. and Hayden, A. (eds.). *The Routledge Handbook of Global Sustainability Governance*. London: Routledge, 296–307.

Fuchs, D. and Lorek, S. 2005. Sustainable Consumption Governance: A History of Promises and Failures. *Journal of Consumer Policy* 28: 261–288.

Fuchs, D., Lorek, S., Di Giulio, A. and Defila, R. 2019. Sources of Power for Sustainable Consumption: Where to Look. In: Martiskainen, M., Middlemiss, L. and Isenhour, C. (eds.). *Power and Politics in Sustainable Consumption Research and Practice*. London: Routledge, 62–83.

Fuchs, D., Schlipphak, B., Treib, O., Nguyen Long, L. A. and Lederer, M. 2020. Which Way Forward in Measuring the Quality of Life? A Critical Analysis of Sustainability and Wellbeing Indicator Sets. *Global Environmental Politics* 20(2): 12–36. doi.org/10.1162/glep_a_00554.

References 87

Godin, L., Laakso, S. and Sahakian, M. 2020. Doing Laundry in Consumption Corridors: Wellbeing and Everyday Life. *Sustainability: Science, Practice and Policy* 16(1): 99–113. doi.org/10.1080/15487733.2020.1785095.
Gough, I. 2017. *Heat, Greed and Human Need: Climate Change, Capitalism and Sustainable Wellbeing.* Cheltenham: Edward Elgar.
Gough, I. 2020. Defining Floors and Ceilings: The Contribution of Human Needs Theory. *Sustainability: Science, Practice, and Policy* 16(1): 208–219. doi.org/10.1080/15487733.2020.1814033.
Grubler, A., Wilson, C., Bento, N., Boza-Kiss, B., Krey, V., McCollum, D. L., Rao, N. D., Riahi, K., Rogelj, J., De Stercke, S., Cullen, J., Frank, S., Fricko, O., Guo, F., Gidden, M., Havlik, P., Huppmann, D., Kiesewetter, G., Rafaj, P., Schoepp, W. and Valin, H. 2018. A Low Energy Demand Scenario for Meeting the 1.5°C Target and Sustainable Development Goals without Negative Emission Technologies. *Nature Energy* 3(6): 515–527.
Guillen-Royo, M. 2010. Realising the 'Wellbeing Dividend': An Exploratory Study using the Human Scale Development Approach. *Ecological Economics* 70(2): 384–393.
Guillen-Royo, M., Guardiola, J. and Garcia-Quero, F. 2017. Sustainable Development in Times of Economic Crisis: A Needs-based Illustration from Granada (Spain). *Journal of Cleaner Production* 150: 267–276.
Institute for Global Environmental Strategies (IGES), Aalto University, and D-mat ltd. 2019. *1.5-Degree Lifestyles: Targets and Options for Reducing Lifestyle Carbon Footprints.* Technical Report. Hayama: Institute for Global Environmental Strategies.
IPCC. 2018. *Global Warming of 1.5°C: An IPCC Special Report on the Impacts of Global Warming of 1.5°C above Pre-industrial Levels and Related Global Greenhouse Gas Emission Pathways, in the Context of Strengthening the Global Response to the Threat of Climate Change, Sustainable Development, and Efforts to Eradicate Poverty.* Geneva: World Meteorological Organization 2018.
Jackson, T. 2005. Live Better by Consuming Less? Is There a "Double Dividend" in Sustainable Consumption? *Journal of Industrial Ecology* 9(1–2): 19–36.
Jackson, T. 2017. *Prosperity without Growth: Foundations for the Economy of Tomorrow.* New York: Routledge.
Jäger-Erben, M., Blättel-Mink, B., Fuchs, D., Götz, K., Langen, N. and Rau, H. Forthcoming. *Grenzen des Konsums im Lebensverlauf: Gelegenheiten, Hürden und Gestaltungsspielräume.* GAIA.
Jolibert, C., Paavola, J. and Rauschmayer, F. 2014. Addressing Needs in the Search for Sustainable Development: A Proposal for Needs-based Scenario building. *Environmental Values* 23(1): 29–50.
Kollmuss, A. and Agyeman, J. 2002. 'Mind the Gap'. *Environmental Education Research* 8(3): 239–260.
Lebow, V. 1955. Price Competition in 1955. *Journal of Retailing* 31(4): 5–10.
Lettenmeier, M. 2018. *A Sustainable Level of Material Footprint: Benchmark for Designing Ecologically Sustainable Lifestyles* (Doctoral Dissertation), Aalto University, Helsinki.

Lorek, S. and Fuchs, D. 2018. *Why it Needs Strong Sustainable Consumption Governance to Achieve Security and Equality in a Sustainable Future.* Paper presented at the World Social Science Forum, Fukuoka, Japan, 25–28 September 2018.

Lorek, S. and Spangenberg, J. 2001. Indicators for Environmentally Sustainable Household Consumption. *International Journal of Sustainable Development* 4(1): 101–120.

Lorek, S. and Spangenberg, J. 2019. *Identification of Promising Instruments and Instrument Mixes to Promote Energy Sufficiency.* EUFORIE – European Futures for Energy Efficiency.

Maniates, M. 2001. Individualization: Plant a Tree, Buy a Bike, Save the World? *Global Environmental Politics* 1(3): 31–52.

Maniates, M. 2019. Beyond Magical Thinking. In Kalfagianni, A., Fuchs, D. and Hayden, A. (eds.). *Routledge Handbook of Global Sustainability Governance.* London: Routledge, 267–281.

Maslow, A. H. 1943. A Theory of Human Motivation. *Psychological Review* 50(4): 370–396.

Max-Neef, M. 1991. *Human-Scale Development: Conception, Application and Further Reflection.* London: Apex Press.

Max-Neef, M., Elizalde, A. and Hopenhayn, M. 1991. Development and Human Needs. In: Max-Neef, M. (ed.). *Human Scale Development: Conception, Application and Further Reflections.* London: Zed Books, 13–54.

Meadows, D. H., Meadows, D. L., Randers, J. and Behrens, W. W. III. 1972. *The Limits to Growth: A Report to the Club of Rome.* New York: Universe Books.

Millward-Hopkins, J., Steinberger, J., Rao, N. and Oswald, Y. 2020. Providing Decent Living with Minimum Energy: A Global Scenario. *Global Environmental Change* 65: 102168. doi:10.1016/j.gloenvcha.2020.102168.

Moser, S. and Kleinhückelkotten, S. 2018. Good Intents, But Low Impacts: Diverging Importance of Motivational and Socioeconomic Determinants Explaining Pro-environmental Behavior, Energy Use, and Carbon Footprint. *Environment and Behavior* 50(6): 626–656.

Muraca, B. and Döring, R. 2018. From (Strong) Sustainability to Degrowth: A Philosophical and Historical Reconstruction. In: Caradonna, J. (ed.). *Routledge Handbook of the History of Sustainability.* London: Routledge, 339–361.

Neuhäuser, C. 2018. *Reichtum als moralisches Problem.* Berlin: Suhrkamp.

Nussbaum, M. 1992. Human Functioning and Social Justice: In Defense of Aristotelian Essentialism. *Political Theory* 20(2): 202–246.

Opschoor, J. 1987. *Duurzaamheid en verandering: over Ecologische inpasbaarheid van Economische ontwikkelingen.* Oratie, Amsterdam: VU Boekhandel/Uitgeverij.

Ottaviani, F. 2018. Time in the Development of Indicators on Sustainable Wellbeing: A Local Experiment in Developing Alternative Indicators. *Social Indicators Research* 135(1): 53–73.

Perry, M. 2016. New US Homes Today are 1,000 Square Feet Larger than in 1973 and Living Space per Person Has Nearly Doubled. AEI Ideas, 5 June. http://www.aei.org/publication/new-us-homes-today-are-1000-square-feet-larger-than-in-1973-and-living-space-per-person-has-nearly-doubled.

Pinsker, J. 2019. Are McMansions Making People Any Happier? *The Atlantic*, 11 June.

Princen, T. 1997. The Shading and Distancing of Commerce: When Internalization is Not Enough. *Ecological Economics* 20(3): 235–253.

Rao, N. D. and Min, J. 2018. Decent Living Standards: Material Prerequisites for Human Wellbeing. *Social Indicators Research* 138: 225–244. doi.org/10.1007/s11205-017-1650-0.

Raworth, K. 2017. A Doughnut for the Anthropocene: Humanity's Compass in the 21st Century. *The Lancet Planetary Health* 1(2): 48–49. doi.org/10.1016/S2542-5196(17)30028-1.

Robeyns, I. 2005. Selecting Capabilities for Quality of Life Measurement. *Social Indicators Research* 74: 191–215. doi.org/10.1007/s11205-005-6524-1.

Rockström, J., Steffen, W., Noone, K., Persson, Å., Chapin, F. S., Lambin, E. F., Lenton, T. M., Scheffer, M., Folke, C., Schellnhuber, H. J., Nykvist, B., de Wit, C. A., Hughes, T., van der Leeuw, S., Rodhe, H., Sörlin, S., Snyder, P. K., Costanza, R., Svedin, U., Falkenmark, M., Karlberg, L., Corell, R. W., Fabry, V. J., Hansen, J., Walker, B., Liverman, D., Richardson, K., Crutzen, P. and Foley, J. A. 2009. A Safe Operating Space for Humanity. *Nature* 461(7263): 472–475.

Røpke, I. 1999. The Dynamics of Willingness to Consume. *Ecological Economics* 28(3): 399–420.

Sahakian, M. 2017. Constructing Normality through Material and Social Lock-in: The Dynamics of Energy Consumption among Geneva's More Affluent Households. In: Hui, A., Day, R. and Walker, G. (eds.). *Demanding Energy: Space, Time and Change*. Cham: Palgrave Macmillan, 51–71.

Sahakian, M. 2019. 'More, Bigger, Better' Household Appliances: Contesting Normativity in Practices through Emotions. *Journal of Consumer Culture* first online, doi.org/10.1177/1469540519889983.

Sahakian, M. and Anantharaman, M. 2020. What Space for Public Parks in Consumption Corridors? Conceptual Reflections on Need Satisfaction through Social Practices. *Sustainability: Science, Practice and Policy* 16:1, 128–142, DOI: 10.1080/15487733.2020.1788697.

Sahakian, M., Anantharaman, M., Di Giulio, A., Saloma, C., Zhang, D., Khanna, R., Narasimalu, S., Favis, A. M., Alfiler, C. A., Narayanan, S., Gao, X. and Li, C. 2020. Green Public Spaces in the Cities of South and Southeast Asia: Protecting Needs Towards Sustainable Wellbeing. *Journal of Public Space* 5: 89–110.

Schor, J. 1998. *The Overspent American: Why We Buy What We Don't Need*. New York: Basic Books.

Schor, J. 2000. *Do Americans Shop Too Much?* New York: Beacon Press.

Sen, A. 1997. *Choice, Welfare and Measurement*. Boston, MA: Harvard University Press.

Sen, A. 2010. *The Idea of Justice*. New York: Penguin.

Shove, E. 2010. Beyond the ABC: Climate Change Policy and Theories of Social Change. *Environmental and Planning A* 42: 1273–1285.

Shove, E. 2018. What is Wrong with Energy Efficiency? *Building Research & Information* 46(7): 779–789.

Shove, E. and Warde, A. 2002. Inconspicuous Consumption: The Sociology of Consumption, Lifestyles and Environment. In: Dunlap, R., Buttel, F., Dickens, P. and Gijswijt, A. (eds.). *Sociological Theory and the Environment*. Lanham, MD: Rowman & Littlefield, 230–251.

Spangenberg, J. 2002. Environmental Space and the Prism of Sustainability: Frameworks for Indicators Measuring Sustainable Development. *Ecological Indicators* 2: 295–309.

Spivak, G. C. 1988. *Can the Subaltern Speak? Reflections on the History of an Idea*. Basingstoke: Macmillan.

Stern, D. 2020. How Large is the Economy-wide Rebound Effect? *Energy Policy* 147: 111870. doi:10.1016/j.enpol.2020.111870.

Stiglitz, J. E., Sen, A. and Fitoussi, J. 2010. *Mismeasuring Our Lives*. New York: New Press.

Victor, P. 2008. *Managing without Growth: Slower by Design, not Disaster*. Cheltenham: Edward Elgar.

Walker G, Simcock, N. and Day, R. 2016. Necessary Energy Uses and a Minimally-decent Standard of Living in the UK: Energy Justice or Escalating Expectations? *Energy Research & Social Science* 18: 129–138.

Wiedmann, T., Lenzen, M., Keyßer, L. and Steinberger, J. 2020. Scientists' Warning on Affluence. *Nature Communications* 11: 3107. doi:10.1038/s41467-020-16941-y.

Wilhite, H. 2016. *The Political Economy of Low Carbon Transformation: Breaking the Habits of Capitalism, Routledge Studies in Low Carbon Development*. London: Routledge.

Index

.

Printed in the United States
by Baker & Taylor Publisher Services